Corporate Cybersecurity

Corporate Cybersecurity

Identifying Risks and the Bug Bounty Program

John Jackson

Registered Office(s)
John Wiley & Sons, Inc., 111 River Street, Hoboken, NJ 07030, USA
John Wiley & Sons Ltd, The Atrium, Southern Gate, Chichester, West Sussex, PO19 8SQ, UK

Editorial Office
The Atrium, Southern Gate, Chichester, West Sussex, PO19 8SQ, UK

For details of our global editorial offices, customer services, and more information about Wiley products visit us at www.wiley.com.

Wiley also publishes its books in a variety of electronic formats and by print-on-demand. Some content that appears in standard print versions of this book may not be available in other formats.

Library of Congress Cataloging-in-Publication Data
Names: Jackson, John (Cybersecurity professional), author.
Title: Corporate cybersecurity : identifying risks and the bug bounty
    program / John Jackson.
Description: Hoboken, NJ : John Wiley & Sons, 2021. | Includes
    bibliographical references and index.
Identifiers: LCCN 2021020794 (print) | LCCN 2021020795 (ebook) |
    ISBN 9781119782520 (hardback) | ISBN 9781119782568 (ebook) |
    ISBN 9781119782537 (pdf) | ISBN 9781119782544 (epub)
Subjects: LCSH: Business enterprises--Computer networks--Security measures. |
    Penetration testing (Computer security) | Cyberspace--Security measures.
Classification: LCC HD30.38 .J34 2021 (print) | LCC HD30.38 (ebook) |
    DDC 658.4/78--dc23
LC record available at https://lccn.loc.gov/2021020794
LC ebook record available at https://lccn.loc.gov/2021020795

Cover image: © WhataWin/Shutterstock
Cover design by Wiley

Set in 9.5/12pt STIX Two Text by Integra Software Services Pvt. Ltd, Pondicherry, India

Printed and bound by CPI Group (UK) Ltd, Croydon, CR0 4YY

C9781119782520_041021

Contents

Foreword

It's safe to say that information security and the industry surrounding it has exploded into a massive, constantly growing sector around the world. Like many other professions within technology, the main attribute which has secured many organizations success (or failure) in maintaining their relevance has been their ability to adapt. In the case of security, we are constantly adapting to methods used by malicious actors with the hopes of becoming as secure as possible – with the goal of identifying (and remediating) vulnerabilities prior to an attack.

As security professionals we understand that it isn't a matter of *if* an event happens, but *when*. Although nothing can be completely secure, it's our job to work towards obtaining a level of maturity within our security programs that are proactive against potential threats. Although zero days will always exist, it's our job to stay up to date and as protected as possible, which can be very costly, especially for many organizations that don't fully understand security and (in many situations) are hesitant to move forward with a proper budget for what is needed to enable adequate professionally accepted levels of protection.

Information security, or cybersecurity, is still in its infancy. This may be a shocking statement to someone who doesn't work within the industry; it is, however, accurate. Only recently have many universities begun offering degrees in the field of cybersecurity. Many pieces of software that would be considered a "must have" for a company's defense in depth weren't in existence just a couple of short years ago.

Many professionals in the industry have moved to their positions as security specialists after previously working in general information technology. I have worked with many organizations, in both the private and the public sectors, and at this point in time, from what I've witnessed, a very small fraction of security professionals have been formally educated in security, and rely heavily on certifications to prove their understanding of the field. This is a blessing for those who need to obtain credentials quickly without the slow drag of the many years of college, but also is a curse for those with certifications but little real world experience. An overwhelming number of professionals are learning on the job, which can be daunting given the fact that many organizations are looking to increase their maturity as quickly as possible.

There are many gears turning in a proper security program. There's an overall lack of understanding of security by those outside of the security team, so one of the most prominent procedures by security professionals is to understand how to assign tasks to the limited resources they have while properly managing a security program that grows in maturity on a constant basis. All in a world where new vulnerabilities can be found daily.

It's no secret that software security and web application security are fast-growing segments within the field of cybersecurity. Every organization has a web presence. Every organization uses software. Individuals also use software and web applications in their daily lives, assets which hold personally identifiable information, and whose contents can greatly range in sensitivity.

Although identifying vulnerabilities through continuous testing is a powerful activity, many organizations don't have the resources or budget to consider it as an option. In search for a remedy to this situation, I have seen many explore the option of creating or joining a bug bounty program, albeit reasons for considering such a program are not limited to such issues. This can clearly be seen in large organizations' involvement with their own bug bounty programs. It's quickly becoming a standard for many large companies to have a bug bounty program, either in house or through a third party.

Bug bounty programs may be new, but they have caught on quickly with proactive organizations seeking to be more secure. It was only in 2013 (less than a decade as of this writing) that Katie Moussouris created Microsoft's first bug bounty program. In March 2016, Moussouris would also be involved with the creation of the Department of Defense's "Hack the Pentagon" pilot program, which would serve as the United States Federal Government's first bug bounty program. Bug bounty programs have gained in popularity due to their benefits greatly outweighing their negatives, many of which are explained clearly within this book, which at the time of writing is geared to be the first wide-release publication on how to create and manage a bug bounty program.

This book is a critical asset for security professionals who seek to understand how to build and operate a bug bounty program. Security professionals can use this book as a guide for the creation of their own bug bounty program. Professionals across all domains of security can use this book to quickly absorb the years of information acquired by real world experience to understand the subject and provide more value to their team.

Robert (@rej_ex) Willis

Acknowledgments

There are far too many influential people in my career to mention in this section. I'm thankful for all of the information security individuals who have let me learn alongside them, given me opportunities, and have put my skills to the test. I've learned many lessons along the way.

A special thank-you to my friend Christian Bobadilla is in order. Christian is one of the most talented application security experts I know, and his humility keeps him out of the information security limelight. Through me, your excellent advice and mentoring lives. If it weren't for you, I wouldn't know even a quarter of what I do about bug bounty programs. Thank you for being a positive role model in my life. It's exceedingly difficult to find people who are not only intellectually sharp and humble but also incredible leaders. This book is dedicated to the faith that you have put in my abilities.

One final dedication: to my father, who encouraged me to try my best at all times. Rest in peace.

Part 1

Bug Bounty Overview

1

The Evolution of Bug Bounty Programs

1.1 Making History

Understanding the evolution of bug bounty programs first requires familiarity with the hacking landscape, or as many in the information security field know it, penetration testing. Security researchers haven't always been respected or given the opportunity to shine. Throughout history, hacking has been a word that scares the public and creates waves of fear inside a company when rumors of a "hack" spread. The first bounty paid for breaking into something (in recorded history) was in 1851. Charles Alfred Hobbs was paid roughly the equivalent of $20,000 to pick a physical lock. (https://www.itspmagazine.com/itsp-chronicles/history-and-interesting-facts-about-bug-bounties-an-appsec-usa-2017-panel-recap).

The first actual bounty program was run by Netscape and it began in 1995. The primary scope was application testing for Netscape Navigator 2.0., their primary product. Slowly, other enterprises started to adapt their own bug bounty programs and offer awards. Bug bounty crowdsourcing platforms introduced the new wave, compiling enterprise programs into a neat catalogue in which security researchers could hop into various programs and begin to participate. Bugcrowd was known as the first crowdsourcing platform in bug bounty history and has been a key player in enterprise bug bounty program management. The pioneers – Casey Ellis, Chris Raethke, and Sergei Belokamen – believed in connecting latent potential to unmet demand with the overall goal of making security easier for everyone. In addition, Ellis firmly believed in assisting security researchers in keeping their records clean. Casey Ellis has also expressed a desire to help educate the youth toward the idea of ethical hacking, rather than a life of crime, and part of the inspiration for creating such a company has to do with the ideal of destigmatizing security research.

In all actuality, reviewing the state and history of bug bounty programs gives the reader a valuable positive perspective, but enterprises are slow to adapt. Even since 1995, there are still fewer than 400 bug bounty programs and 1600 vulnerability disclosure programs that exist in the world. The surprisingly small number of programs that exist in the world represent the resistance and conservatism of the field of legal hacking, otherwise known as security research.

Corporate Cybersecurity: Identifying Risks and the Bug Bounty Program, First Edition. John Jackson.
© 2021 John Wiley & Sons, Ltd. Published 2021 by John Wiley & Sons, Ltd.

1.2   Conservative Blockers

When information security specialists learn about bug bounty programs, many of them are excited to get involved. Application security is a growing field, and modern day web, mobile, and hardware assets need to be protected. With such an essential requirement to protect applications, enterprises still resist the absolute necessity of making vulnerability reporting management a prioritized incentive. As with everything, there's not a "one-size-fits-all" answer for why an enterprise would ignore application security; however, many factors play a role in the resistance that is widespread, even today. For example, here are some of the reasons a company may decide to ignore the idea of a bug bounty program:

- Increased threat actor activity.
- Security researchers scamming.
- Applications being a small consideration.
- Enormous budgetary requirements.
- Other security tooling as a priority.

There are obviously several other reasons an enterprise may believe a bug bounty program will cause unnecessary risk or negative effects. Debunking the above five defined points will give people a better understanding of why being afraid is natural, but it can be detrimental to the overall health of a good application security program.

1.3   Increased Threat Actor Activity

An enterprise may be fearful that establishing a bug bounty program will cause an increase of malicious threat actors attempting to hack into or successfully exploiting applications. The logic can be portrayed as such, "If an enterprise bug bounty program is established, then security researchers will be allowed to hack, and it will be impossible to tell who is malicious." The problem with this statement's assumption that threat actors are hiding among security researchers is one of a common philosophical logical fallacy: the Slippery Slope.

The Slippery Slope logical fallacy is best defined as, "A course of action that seems to lead inevitably from one action or result in another with unintended consequences." In layman's terms, the translation of the Slippery Slope in the security research scenario is, "If the enterprise allows security researchers to conduct research, we will be maliciously exploited." It's best to imagine the scenario of increased threat actor activity with the other perspective in mind. Without a bug bounty program, flaws may never be identified – vulnerabilities that could compromise an organization's sensitive information or intellectual property.

Enterprises considering operating bug bounty programs should learn effective logging and prevention through logging mechanisms and web application firewalls, which are discussed later in this book.

1.4   Security Researcher Scams

Any type of business that relies on services rendered by another party should always be weary of scamming. Understanding the vulnerability types, criticality, and assessing payment amounts will always be the best course of action for a company running a bug bounty program. Still, the idea of scamming isn't a new one. Potential program managers have to learn best practices and understand the basics of vulnerability management. Nonetheless, protections for programs are in place. Managed services offered through bug bounty crowd-sourcing platforms such as Bugcrowd and HackerOne will become useful tools. The triage team will assist in validating the legitimacy of a vulnerability which can assist in preventing scamming. Program managers shouldn't solely rely on the validation, but scamming happens far more infrequently than enterprises that are on the fence imagine.

1.5   Applications Are a Small Consideration

Enterprises that avoid bug bounty programs because of the idea of applications being a small attack surface are asking for trouble. When employees tasked with the security of a company evaluate vulnerability potential, the obvious go-to is to secure the network and related assets. However, web and mobile applications in particular have become exceedingly complex. With multiple development languages and servers, the attack surface is far greater than one might imagine. Consider the following example:

Server → Hosts one part of the web application → One assigned IP address
Web application → Connected to multiple servers → Multiple IP addresses

The deployment of an enterprise's assets will always be the determinant factor in the attack service; however, modern applications are becoming more interconnected than they ever were in the past. It's easy to think about a "server" as an asset with a wide attack surface, and in many cases, that is true, and the attack vectors will always vary. Regardless, enterprises should not consider the value of a bug bounty program as something minute and ineffective. In addition, flawed application logic may result in the exploitation of the network and enterprises may not consider that. For example, SQL (Structured Query Language) injection can result in a full server-database dump or remote code execution on the network. Server side request forgery can result in the exposure of sensitive information leading to unauthorized server access or pivoting to other parts of the network. Application security is a large undertaking and neglecting it can result in the full compromise of an enterprise.

1.6   Enormous Budgetary Requirements

Bug bounty programs scale. The size and operation of the bug bounty program is up to the enterprise to decide. In addition, if the company isn't giant, it's unrealistic to assume that the enterprise would have to pay a large sum of money to get a program up and running.

With bug bounty crowdsourcing becoming the norm, companies like Bugcrowd and HackerOne are willing to have scoping calls with leadership to identify a fair pricing model for program management. The price of program management is well worth the cost of identifying vulnerabilities that can result in the loss of hundreds of thousands, if not millions, of dollars in assets or compliance violations such as GDPR (General Data Protection Regulation) or the California Privacy Act. Application security, like any other subbranch of security, is an investment – and security doesn't typically see hefty returns on investment. Information security doesn't make a company money: it protects the company from losing money, allowing the acquisition of money.

1.7 Other Security Tooling as a Priority

Out of all of the other potential worries for setting up a program, security tooling is a legitimate concern. Balancing a budget requires coordination with all levels of leadership and an overall evaluation of security posture. For example, establishing a bug bounty program isn't likely a good idea if the enterprise does not have a web application firewall, or a decent endpoint protection and response solution. Coordination with the security team will have to occur, but if all other bases are covered, there's no reason a basic bug bounty program cannot be established.

1.8 Vulnerability Disclosure Programs vs. Bug Bounty Programs

Even for the most technical of individuals, understanding the difference between a vulnerability disclosure program (VDP) and a bug bounty program (BBP) can be mind boggling. Even still, engineers who run bug bounty programs may make the mistake over calling a bug bounty program a vulnerability disclosure program, or vice versa. Understanding the difference between the two is essential to communicating expectations clearly and educating the general public on the day-to-day processes involved.

1.8.1 Vulnerability Disclosure Programs

Vulnerability disclosure programs are the method used when an enterprise wants to facilitate the disclosure of vulnerabilities but not offer any sort of paid incentive. Vulnerability disclosure programs can be considered a goodwill type of vulnerability management process. The two types of vulnerability disclosure programs are managed and unmanaged. An unmanaged program would be a vulnerability disclosure program that is offered in-house, with an associated good faith based effort. In contrast, a managed vulnerability disclosure program could be one where program managers are assisted by a triage team from a bug bounty crowdsourcing platform such as Bugcrowd or HackerOne. As an incentive to researchers, they are offered points in return for reports, which is an essential part of leveling-up and getting invited to private programs, which typically have less competition for security researchers and a better chance of vulnerability finding.

Private vulnerability disclosure programs are also allowed through crowdsourcing platforms, reducing the costs associated with paying bounties as points will be rewarded.

1.8.2 Bug Bounty Programs

Bug bounty programs are typically more mature vulnerability disclosure programs, offering rewards in place of points. When program managers want to convert their vulnerability disclosure programs to bug bounty programs, the process is typically as simple as initiating a financial incentive for security research. Bug bounty programs carry more weight and attract more professional hackers. For example, some of the best security researchers may never participate in vulnerability disclosure programs because the time they spend evaluating bug bounty programs could easily be time converted to a cash flow. An enterprise's end state should always be aspiring to reach paid-program participation. Security research consumes a lot of time and an enterprise should want to pay its researchers for the time spent. If confused, think of it like this: how many people are willing to do a full-time job for free versus paid? Hobbyists will always exist, but the participation of some of the greatest security researchers can only be obtained with monetary incentives.

1.9 Program Managers

Throughout the book, the phrase "program manager" will come up frequently. A program manager isn't to be thought of as a traditional manager who coordinates employee activity. Rather, program managers are any employee who deals with the configuration or management of an enterprise bug bounty program. For example, the title of the employee doesn't matter: an application security engineer or a chief information security officer could be a program manager. The only consideration is that the employee must have oversight of the program and the ability to make changes. After all, even an employee who is remediating bugs is managing the day-to-day workflow of the program.

1.10 The Law

Historically, the law hasn't always been kind to security researchers. Even today, hacking is still considered dangerous or controversial to nontechnical people. A substantial part of society does not view hacking as an art, but as a criminal behavior in all circumstances. When most people view hacking as an overwhelmingly criminal activity, it is unsurprising that legitimate researchers often find themselves working in a hostile environment, and one that threatens to punish them. Many documented instances of security researchers being threatened with legal action exist. A quick search on the Internet of the phrase "security researcher threatened" will bring up quite a bit of news.

Redefining the expectations of security research starts with educating the community – and bug bounty programs play a gigantic role in helping society understand that hacking can be ethical. Vulnerability disclosure programs are a great start, but the end state is a transition to a bug bounty program that allows hackers to receive fair compensation for their efforts. Nonetheless, security research without utilizing a bug bounty program can be highly dangerous and can risk the livelihood of the individual conducting the research. A bug bounty program and the safe harbor clauses it contains can help to guarantee researcher safety. Vulnerability research has changed the landscape of what category hackers fall into, and has allowed quite a bit of flexibility and protection from punishment from the law.

1.11   Redefining Security Research

During the course of this book, the reader will see what skills are necessary to create, manage, and refine bug bounty programs. The one important aspect to remember when reading this book is that establishing or managing a bug bounty program is only one small part of a much bigger picture. History is being made, in real time, and the expansion of ethical hacking into the enterprise space is a necessary component of ensuring the safety of company assets and user data. Understanding how important programs can be is a way of information security that should be shared in a positive light. The best way to bring attention to the ethical nature of thousands of security researchers while they hack and make a difference is to operate with an open mind and attempt to give honest disclosure, while awarding processes a fair evaluation on every occasion.

Security research, or in other words the art of hacking, needs the assistance of enterprises that operate bug bounty programs – to adequately reshape the landscape of hacking. As a community, we cannot let the fear of hacking prevail as the action of shaming individuals that care about the security of an organization ends up causing more harm than good. Reshaping the world will take the cooperation and understanding of all individuals involved in the process. In addition, enterprises should maintain a neutral state of mind. Security researchers hack for various reasons: money, credibility, press, portfolio building, or fun. The reason vulnerability research is conducted should hardly matter: the only responsibility of the enterprise is to provide a safe environment and to patch the vulnerabilities. Fear of the press, while a legitimate concern, can be redirected into positive energy that rewards and values the researchers. If the organization engages openly with the researcher, it could well result in a positive outcome, in terms of media spin or as a learning outcome.

1.12   Taking Action

It shouldn't come as a surprise that word of mouth is a powerful tool. The enterprise space is ever-expansive and companies will constantly compete to be better than their competition. As a society, the establishment of honest programs and disclosure processes can influence the entire enterprise space. Here are some ways program managers or potential program managers can help assist researchers and the security research space.

1.12.1   Get to Know Security Researchers

Be involved in the community aspect of research. Whether reading publications on CVEs (common vulnerabilities and exposures) or bug writeups, participating in Twitter conversations, or connecting with hackers on LinkedIn, it's important to understand all aspects of the landscape.

1.12.2   Fair and Just Resolution

Running a program isn't the final solution. Managing an enterprise program requires collaboration and fair resolution processes. Ensuring that the program stays ethical and cares about the security researchers is a key part of spreading the positive aspects of bug bounty programs.

1.12.3   Managing Disclosure

While not recommended until a program is more established, eventually enterprises should strive to help researchers disclose their findings to the public when patched, if they wish to do so. Research disclosure helps inspire new generations of hackers and also receives enterprise, and potentially media, attention. Nonetheless, within a program security researchers should maintain the ability to disclose in any circumstance if the information is redacted enough or if a CVE exists on an enterprise product/there's user or customer PII exposure that needs to go public.

1.12.4   Corrections

Program managers should strive to speak highly of researchers and the great work that is provided as a service. "Hackers" aren't malicious by default, and program managers receive first-hand experience of ethical behavior. When hackers are called malicious, program managers should strive to set the record straight and describe the differences between an ethical hacker (security researcher) and a malicious hacker (threat actor).

1.12.5   Specific Community Involvement

Joining the movement for better disclosure is the first step to a greater collaboration between researchers and programs. Casey Ellis built a one-of-a-kind community named Disclose as a way for companies to participate in the conversation. (https://disclose.io).

Part 2

Evaluating Programs

2

Assessing Current Vulnerability Management Processes

2.1 Who Runs a Bug Bounty Program?

Ultimately, who would be responsible for starting a bug bounty program? Ideally, a bug bounty program manager should be whoever does the day-to-day work in coordinated application or web application security measures.

Not every engineer has the dilemma of figuring out their role in the vulnerability management process. If an engineer is hired as an application security engineer, it's a given that they will have to be responsible for monitoring and triaging any application vulnerabilities as they pertain to mobile or web applications. It's important to understand that engineers who have the sole responsibility of vulnerability management typically focus on network vulnerabilities. It would be unusual to see a security engineer on the vulnerability management team identify, remediate, or manage application vulnerabilities.

The ideal situation is one in which an application security manager and at least one application security or general security engineer set up and manage a bug bounty program. However, this isn't always the case. Therefore, it's important to have the tools to know what to do if it's your responsibility to establish a program.

2.2 Determining Security Posture

The most difficult part of the entire process of executing a bug bounty program for an enterprise is evaluating the risk and risk mitigation programs. While a reader may not be a compliance expert, or an endpoint detection and response engineer, determining which role that will have to be played in the vulnerability management process is nonnegotiable. The position that an engineer was hired to fill at the company will directly assist one in understanding what specific expectations lie ahead.

"Security posture" is a flexible term. Truthfully, it would be impossible to recommend an in-depth and thorough analysis without understanding what type of business use case is in play. Risk analysis requires visualizing how all of the parts of a security team come together, and rationally determining how it plays into application security. As a rule of thumb, it can be evaluated from the perspective of management or engineering. While there are many

Corporate Cybersecurity: Identifying Risks and the Bug Bounty Program, First Edition. John Jackson.
© 2021 John Wiley & Sons, Ltd. Published 2021 by John Wiley & Sons, Ltd.

other aspects and subcategories of information security, a fair baseline will be starting with understanding some of the core differences in responsibility as they pertain to management and engineering:

2.3 Management

It wouldn't be absurd to suggest that an application security manager is typically responsible for evaluating the connections between the product and the application security team, and other departments in the organization. It's the manager's job to choose the right personnel to ensure the successful day-to-day operation of the enterprise. After operational pace is established, a manager has to determine which appropriate remediation steps need to occur before creating a bug bounty program. In the application security realm, vulnerability remediation communication occurs between a wide range of groups. As a baseline here are some of the teams that a manager will have to collaborate with.

2.3.1 Software Engineering Teams

Responsible for the development of the applications that will be subject to testing when a bug bounty program is established.

2.3.2 Security Departments (Security Operations, Fraud Prevention, Governance/Risk/Compliance, Edge Controls, Vulnerability Management, Endpoint Detection, and Response)

The various subteams that make up the root of security, subject to be vastly different based on the structure of the organization.

2.3.3 Infrastructure Teams

Responsible for the backbone of the organization that is meant for hosting applications and various assets that both stakeholders and users/customers operate.

2.3.4 Legal Department

Application security managers may have to communicate with the legal department if malicious activity is noted. Therefore, managers should have close relationships with legal representatives.

2.3.5 Communications Team

Depending on the structure of the organization, social media marketing may be up to the communications or marketing teams. Researchers may reach out via social media to disclose vulnerabilities and application security managers should be aware of this, and adequately prepare the responsible team.

2.4   Important Questions

It's crucial to keep in mind that the answers to some of the questions covered in this section may be trivial. If known, that's absolutely fantastic! When the answers are not known, future program managers may be able to find out without disrupting the team or space. Managers should make an effort to be cordial and responsive to concerns or pushback. It's always better to know than to assume: operating in a presumptuous way can open the door to security issues or ineffective vulnerability management processes. In reality, the questions that proceed are to be used as a baseline and not as a full representation of an enterprise risk management guide.

During the processes of identifying risk, application security managers will find that many other questions arise – that's great! Ask them! Operating in a way that creates a dialogue between the various teams and application security is a great first step toward building rapport and trust. Maintaining trust is an essential part of securing the organization, as it is impossible to remediate vulnerabilities if other teams do not trust the remediation techniques that will be placed by the application security team. While it may not initially be possible to understand how every single team works together, application security is most effective when an application security manager can envision the macrovision of enterprise security. In addition, application security managers should avoid siloing off and exercising an "unreachable" state. The resolution of vulnerabilities can occur twice as fast if managers know the other major players and innovators within the organization. Here are some questions that can be asked with explanations of why these questions should be answered.

2.5   Software Engineering

2.5.1   Which Processes Are in Place for Secure Coding? Do the Software Engineers Understand the Importance of Mitigating the Risks Associated with Vulnerable Code?

Once again, application security managers should never assume that engineers have a working knowledge of secure coding. The best way to achieve enterprise security is to understand the way software engineers build, and assist in establishing best practice. No organization is perfect. Therefore, it will take time to work with all of the teams that exist in the enterprise. Secure coding platforms such as Checkmarx Codebashing and security awareness incentives such as hacking demos, security riddles, and other fun educational events can help break down any barriers that may exist between application security and software engineering. (https://www.checkmarx.com/products/codebashing-enterprise-application-security-training).

2.5.2   How Effective Are Current Communication Processes? Will Vulnerabilities Be Quickly Resolved If Brought to Their Attention?

Evaluating the communication processes and vulnerability remediation expectations will develop over time. The question of effective communication and resolution isn't one to ask software engineering teams, but it is a matter that should be carefully documented, and reevaluated when more data is available.

2.5.3   Is the Breadth of Our Enterprise's Web and Mobile Applications Immense? Which Processes Are Engineers Using for Development in the Software Development Lifecycle?

In summary, managers should identify how many applications exist and what the software development lifecycle (SDLC) looks like. Preventing vulnerabilities starts with implementing adequate application security processes beforehand.

2.6   Security Departments

2.6.1   How Does Security Operations Manage Incidents? Will Employee Assistance Be Provided from the Security Operations Team If a Threat Actor Manages to Exploit an Application Vulnerability? Which Tools Do They Have in Place?

Incidents are inevitable for any growing organization, and an incident that only affects a security operations team, or an application security team, is unrealistic. Application security managers will have to bridge the communication gap between engineers and management on both teams to collaborate on investigations. Establishing thorough processes in the event of an application incident that ends up affecting both teams (such as a client side web application exploit that turns into a server side exploit) isn't negotiable. Transparency with incident resolution should be maintained between both teams. Application security managers should know what forensic tools, logging solutions, and endpoint detection response tools exist within the enterprise. Many of the tools owned by other security teams can greatly benefit the application security team during investigative or prevention processes. Team collaboration can allow for a togetherness mindset of security instead of a reluctance to provide assistance.

2.6.2   What Does the Fraud Prevention Team Do to Prevent Malicious Activities? How Many Occurrences Do They See of Issues such as Account Takeover, and Could They Potentially Create Application Vulnerabilities?

If a fraud team exists within the enterprise, application security will have a ton of collaboration work to do. For example, the aspects of security that the fraud team focus on are important areas of review for application security as well. If the fraud team sees instances of account takeover, application security engineers will have to brainstorm the prevention methodologies for the login page logic. Alternatively, if the fraud team starts to see a giant spike in gift card purchases, application security may have to review the application security of the gift card purchase and redemption pages to ensure that vulnerabilities do not exist. The possibilities are endless.

2.6.3 Are There Any Compliance Practices in Place and, If So, How Do They Affect the Vulnerability Management Process? What Does the Application Security Team Have to Do to Assist in Enterprise Compliance?

Compliance teams within the organization will have to review third-party security relationships as well as internal security compliance. Application security managers should understand the processes to best help in evaluating and remediating risks that may affect adequate compliance.

2.6.4 What Edge Tooling Is in Place to Prevent Attacks? Are Any of the Enterprise Applications at Risk of Being Exploited due to an IoT (Internet of Things) Device?

IoT is a large attack vector. The security of Internet-connected devices may be up to a dedicated team, such as an edge team, or may fall into the purview of a security operations team. Nonetheless, the exploitation of IoT devices is an important consideration for application security as these devices might directly connect to or host enterprise applications.

2.6.5 How Often Does Our Vulnerability Management Team Push for Updates? How Does the Vulnerability Management Team Ensure Servers in which Enterprise Applications Reside Are Secure?

Vulnerability management processes are complex, and when teams are dedicated to such efforts, the attack surface does end up reduced. However, knowing how the processes are coordinated for resolution is necessary for application security managers. For example, if a security researcher abuses a server identified from the web application because it's out of date, the vulnerability management team will have to assist, and knowing what type of collaboration will need to occur is quite important.

2.7 Infrastructure Teams

2.7.1 What Are Infrastructure Teams Doing to Ensure Best Security Practices Are Enabled? How Long Will It Take the Infrastructure Team to Resolve a Serious Issue When a Server-side Web Application Is Exploited, or During a Subdomain Takeover Vulnerability?

Even though application security isn't responsible for the security of servers, pivots can take place and a researcher may report an exploit to the application security team that involves a server. Application security managers will have to know what the coordination efforts look like to resolve the problem. In addition, collaborating with nonsecurity-oriented teams may prove challenging so it's best to develop effective security practices before issues are identified.

2.7.2 Is There Effective Communication between Infrastructure, Vulnerability Management, Security Operations, and Endpoint Detection and Response?

On some occasions, a vulnerability will end up requiring the attention of many teams. Stressing the importance of security being a team fight, even for nonsecurity-based teams, will be the smoking gun of application security. The sooner teams understand that remediating vulnerabilities must be a priority, the easier collaboration will be.

2.8 Legal Department

2.8.1 How Well Refined is the Relationship between the Application Security Team and the Legal Department?

Transparent communication between application security and the legal department is necessary in the event that application security needs coverage should communications go awry with a security researcher or a threat actor is identified. Application security managers should attempt to build rapport with the legal department immediately.

2.8.2 What Criteria Are/Will Be Set Out for the Escalation of Issues?

Identifying enterprise regulations for the escalation of any identified vulnerabilities is a requirement. For example, the legal department will advise in the event that PII is accessed by a security researcher or an unauthorized threat actor.

2.8.3 Does the Legal Department Understand the Necessity of Bug Bounty Program Management?

If no communications have occurred between the legal department and the application security team, confusion may occur if an application security manager asks for guidance on a possible threat or breach scenario. A weak rapport between application security and the legal department could result in advice that includes threatening a security researcher. Application security managers should make an honest effort to explain to the legal department what bug bounty programs do and how they assist – given that they are not familiar with such processes.

2.9 Communications Team

2.9.1 Has the Communications Team Dealt with Security Researchers Before? Is the Importance Understood?

Asking employees on the communications team if they have dealt with security research is important. If the team has dealt with a security researcher reporting through social media, identify how the communication was carried out. Explaining the importance of adequate and cordial collaboration with a researcher is essential.

2.9.2   Was the Communications Team Informed of Bug Bounty Program Expectations?

Knowing how teams that manage social media intend to deal with a researcher who discloses a vulnerability publicly or through direct message is a key piece of information to have. Application security managers should redefine expectations with the teams to enable a direct line between the application security and communications team.

The importance of asking questions as a manager is to ensure that the enterprise is prepared for all of the vectors of risk before establishing a bug bounty program within the organization. Forging alliances and receiving answers to questions may not be the sole responsibility of management. Application security managers should discuss the risk assessment measures with engineers on the team and other employees in various security departments that may be able to achieve answers, or may even have answers already.

2.10   Engineers

An engineer's primary responsibility is to assist management in determining all of the vulnerabilities and risks that could be directly related to or impact the application security team. It never hurts to ask questions, and arguably some of the best engineers will want to know everything about the process – just as management will. Many engineers that may come across this book will be in a position other than application security and may not be ready to take on the responsibility of a bug bounty program without a manager. If that's the case, it's crucial to review the management section and get a thorough grasp of vulnerability management and how it pertains to application security.

Engineers should care about the passion for the craft and the great contributions that researchers will put forward. Even if a security engineer has management who has put a substantial amount of effort into knowing the entire enterprise layout and application security responsibilities, they should aspire to ingest all of that information. There's not a day that goes by in day-to-day responsibilities in which a security engineer does not need to be familiar with the various enterprise teams and vulnerability remediation best practices.

2.11   Program Readiness

Bug bounty programs are an amazing security tool. A good program can provide valuable insight and help enterprises continuously test their assets. It's important to note that the effectiveness of a program can only be as good as the program manager who configures it. Future program managers should identify telltale signs that their organization may not be ready to start a bug bounty program. As already stated, close communication between the various teams and a precise definition of expectations are essential when setting up a bug bounty program.

Going through the various risk assessment and information gathering processes to define the enterprise security stance is not an option: it's a requirement. Enterprises cannot build a house without a foundation, and avoiding any advance risk-assessment exercises will undoubtedly result in the shoddiest of bug bounty programs. While a bug bounty program can be a useful way to identify vulnerabilities, it isn't the be all and end all, and engineers or managers who go through the process of attempting to set up a program without first evaluating the other aspects of security might burn their enterprise. Recovering is possible, but it would be better to carefully prepare and evaluate security gaps before launching a program. Even a limited bug bounty program can result in frustrated security researchers if communication gaps are not filled in before inviting researchers to participate in a program.

3

Evaluating Program Operations

3.1 One Size Does Not Fit All

Future program managers need to understand how to work with what they have. When it comes to looking at the different options for programs, it's important to remember that one size doesn't fit all. One enterprise may run a successful public program, while another enterprise struggles to do so. The reason there seems to be such a wide variance in appropriate program types is because of the enterprise security model, configurations, and level of flexibility that a program may or may not have. In the application security space, there's a lack of understanding when addressing program configuration, and a careful review during setup will give an enterprise the ability to gather relevant vulnerabilities and manage/resolve these issues effectively. Program managers must understand the key differences in the setup process for maximum success.

An enterprise's bug bounty program is only as good as its reputation. Hackers will consistently engage with the program if they feel that it's representing their needs efficiently. As a starting point, program managers will want to review all aspects of an established program in place and expand or retract as needed. If the enterprise does not have a bug bounty program, the goal to achieve will undoubtedly be to create an effective program from the ground-up.

3.2 Realistic Program Scenarios

In lieu of explaining program options with bullet points and graphs, read the following scenario of an ethical hacker who accidentally discovers a vulnerability, and what the approach would look like from their perspective. Then consider how to explain each option. By doing so, bug bounty program functionality can be better understood.

A hacker is using their favorite website to buy electronics and other home goods. The checkout process appears to be standard. They type in their name, their address, email address, and so on. Now it's time to pay. The hacker enters their card information and submits the request to the server. The standard "thank you for your purchase" message and confirmation number didn't appear. Instead, they received an Internal Server Error (500).

At this point, red flags are flying at full mast. What happened, why is the hacker receiving this message? A hacker's curiosity burns with the power of a thousand suns. The ethical hacker backpedals, carefully reviewing the checkout process. One by one, they decide to

Corporate Cybersecurity: Identifying Risks and the Bug Bounty Program, First Edition. John Jackson.
© 2021 John Wiley & Sons, Ltd. Published 2021 by John Wiley & Sons, Ltd.

test each input field, adding a single quote to the end of the information submitted. They've now managed to replicate a possible SQL (Structured Query Language)injection by adding this single quote to the last name field of the checkout form. They save the POST request in a file, feed it into SQLMap and test the last name parameter. Within seconds they can now dump the entire SQL database and get a reverse shell, accessing every single piece of PII (personally identifiable information) on the company's server. The hacker knows that they can take this even further. The hacker's thoughts are now racing at a million miles per second, and their heart is beating uncontrollably fast. They quietly contemplate and think to themselves, "I'm not a criminal. I need to report this. What if a threat actor decides to exploit this vulnerability with malicious intentions?"

3.3   Ad Hoc Program

An ad hoc program is a program that may not necessarily be considered organized. Many enterprises have a security page where bugs can be reported, or instructions for reporting with a security.txt file hosted on the root domain, and others gamble on the probability of a hacker performing good faith reporting and contacting the company. If the perspective of a security researcher is considered, reporting the vulnerability might be difficult and various circumstances may deter a researcher from doing so. Primarily, even the most seasoned security researchers fear retaliation, and an ad hoc program leaves the floor open for guesswork. Researchers want to do the right thing, but hacking without permission is currently taboo and it leaves a lot to be desired.

With a wide variety of unknown enterprise-to-hacker response possibilities, researchers might avoid reporting vulnerabilities altogether. Assuming that the researcher wants to do the right thing, they will likely first check the website to look for a point of contact for the enterprise's security team. If they don't find anything, they may reach out to the company or security professionals on social media websites, or use a contact form on the website. If an enterprise maintains a new or underdeveloped security posture, or doesn't adequately highlight various ways to get in contact about security issues, vulnerabilities may never be reported.

An enterprise may believe that utilizing a spontaneous reporting methodology seems useful, even foolproof. Unfortunately, it can be dangerous to assume that security researchers will reach the enterprise without any mention of a program. Security researchers come in all shapes and sizes, and from all walks of life. Language barriers and cultural differences may result in reported research that seems malicious or threatening. A company with security professionals that don't understand proper vulnerability management or security research might end up threatening the researcher or reporting them out of fear. As a program manager, being aware of the potential threats that researchers face during disclosure could be a way to ease the pain of reporting.

In addition to a limited ad hoc reporting configuration preventing adequate communication, there are a wide range of vulnerabilities that exist, further complicating the situation. For example, a client side misconfiguration versus a server side misconfiguration might be managed by two completely separate teams. Additionally, a dedicated team to address all client side or server side exploits might be unrealistic. A certain block of servers may end up being managed by one team, and another block of servers managed by another team, and so on and so forth. Standard enterprise models have a lot of applications, servers, components, etc. An enterprise without a dedicated bug bounty program may open up the possibility for a lot of communication issues and misinterpretation, or a lack of understanding can lead to the researcher disclosing to the media, damaging the company's reputation.

Company reputation aside, many bugs can be exploited in critical ways that could negatively impact revenue, customers, clients, and so on. One communication blunder in the research process can result in valuable and legitimate vulnerability findings being lost. Visibility through an established program, reluctance, or withdrawal of a researcher's findings may have negative consequences – and ad hoc programs do not have adequate mediation because of existing biases, whereas a bug bounty platform allows researchers and enterprises to communicate with one another effectively.

It's important to note that, while an ad hoc program may not be for every company, it doesn't mean it's completely ineffective. A smaller company with fewer employees or assets may not warrant the need for an organized third-party program. However, security engineers should keep that in mind and even still quote the cost of creating a third-party bug bounty program. Nonetheless, even if a company decides not to establish a program, they should be prepared to respond to, validate, and reward ad hoc findings in a way that is concise and fair to researchers. After all, while a researcher may not have had permission to test, the vulnerability exists and could lead to full-scale exploitation, irrevocably damaging the enterprise's reputation or resulting in great monetary losses. Having an open mind will utilizing an ad hoc program is an essential part of doing so.

On a positive note, ad hoc programs are the cheapest possible solution. An enterprise should use this program until a baseline security posture is established, especially if they have nothing else. An ad hoc program will always be the cheapest option, but it's apparent that it could take a toll on the communication between a researcher and an enterprise.

An ad hoc program is best defined for an enterprise that has the ability to manage large volumes of vulnerability reports. For example, if an enterprise is too large, they may find better results by offloading most, if not all, of their reporting architecture to a third-party crowdsourced research platform. Large enterprises that care about the state of their security will not offload; otherwise, it could put their data and assets at risk. Imagine if the enterprise in question were an ecommerce site that ran through a web development company. The company that became entrusted with the managing aspects of the enterprises' services would be responsible for the security posture of the web application and the server that hosted the application. An important distinction to make is what the stance on custom application plugins is, as requiring the client to keep plugins updated might be something that would have to be considered. Even if plugins have to be kept up to date, doing so usually won't warrant a full-scale bug bounty program, in comparison to a more standard projected enterprise model. Plugins that are derived from a library of on-demand applications will be maintained by third parties. If researchers find vulnerabilities that affect the applications, it will be considered a zero-day exploit. If reported through MITRE or other appropriate means, a notice will be sent out by the third-party provider (given the appropriate scenario), but an offload to a third-party provider for most of the infrastructure may result in the partner company not informing the company in the event of exploitation, and the enterprise must be vigilant to risks no matter what program model is used.

3.4 Note

This book won't focus on the aspect of setting up custom-built vulnerability disclosure programs or bug bounty programs. The margin for error with the legality of paying researchers through a custom program could open up unnecessary risk, and the objective of this book strays away from any fully custom program setup that utilizes a proprietary platform solution. Without leveraging the extensive features and capacity of a program run through a bug bounty crowdsourcing platform, the overall considerations for vulnerability management become a lot larger. Please exercise caution if setting up a completely in-house solution. Ensure that a risk assessment is performed and that legal agreements are up to date and comply with the local, state, and government laws. If the enterprise has in-house lawyers, consult about potential legal mitigation before setting up the program. Enterprise vulnerability program managers must remember that a completely in-house program may need to extend into the field of compliance as well, owing to researchers who may submit PII or sensitive information such as payment information, home address, and so on, coupled with the required delivery of tax documentation. This book is not a replacement for any form of legal advice, so all and any program should be setup at one's own risk, regardless of the platform used or created.

3.5 Applied Knowledge

3.5.1 Applied Knowledge #1

Imagine if the hacker from our earlier story takes the SQL vulnerability that was identified and searches for a way to report the vulnerability. If they search and find a lack of security email address, they may decide to use the customer support email address instead. Knowing that there's a certain level of fragility with reporting a vulnerability with this much impact, they say something along the lines of:

> Hello,
> My name is X and I'm a hacker. I've found a serious vulnerability that allows someone to obtain credit card information, passwords, addresses, and so on through a simple exploit. Please reply as soon as possible.

Given a realistic scenario, a simple email that expresses the urgency is fairly effective. If a security professional were asked what should be done in the instance of an email as defined above, they would usually recommend that the customer service specialist gather more information or ask a set of questions and then forward the hacker to a specified email address for security purposes.

Unfortunately, that's just not the most realistic approach. Using an ad hoc program, vulnerability management professionals aren't typically coordinating with their customer support team on the bug resolution process. Communication breakdown can open up the possibility of a wide variety of security issues which may hinder the professional resolution of vulnerabilities. As an organization, it feels easy enough to avoid a researcher – but no one has the power to wish away a vulnerability, not even governments or top officials.

3.5.1.1 Private Programs

When an enterprise sets up the baseline security posture, the next step is to harden the environment further. To do so, they typically establish a private bug bounty program. Private programs are the evolution of ad hoc programs. They demonstrate a willingness to commit to rewarding and encouraging active participation. Private programs can be seen as a steppingstone to a wider vulnerability disclosure program.

A private program, compared to an ad hoc program, is a day and night difference. Instead of waiting for researchers to approach the enterprise with vulnerabilities, the responsibility and expectation of the program managers and engineers is to actively seek researchers to participate in their bug bounty program. Similarities will always exist in some researcher intake processes. However, establishing a legitimate program will make it easier to manage ad hoc researchers. Private bug bounty programs facilitate enterprises to manage the flow of hackers and control which assets are tested, and when.

Still, operating a private program comes with its own challenges. For example, a poorly configured, mismanaged, or neglected program can result in the same issues that an ad hoc program results in. If researchers do not feel heard, some will quit, while others won't hesitate to attack the reputation of a company. Neglected programs have similar results. Therefore, it's exceedingly important to remember that just because the program is private doesn't mean that it can tolerate mismanagement.

3.5.2 Applied Knowledge #2

The hacker takes their SQL vulnerability and searches for a way to report the vulnerability. Upon finding no security email address, they decide to use the customer support email address. This scenario differs in one key way. Customer support knows that the enterprise has a team that's responsible for vulnerability management. Customer support quickly forwards the email over to the security team, which notifies the bug bounty program manager. An email can now be sent to the hacker, and they can be onboarded into the private program.

A key takeaway from this applied knowledge scenario is to ensure that the customer support team knows the appropriate point of contact for forwarding vulnerability-related email. As an engineer or a program manager responsible for managing engineers, be proactive. The sooner a meeting is held between the responsible point of contact at customer support and a bug bounty program manager, the easier it will be to deal with all future issues.

3.5.2.1 Public Programs

The most dangerous type of vulnerability disclosure program is a public program, and dangerous here means, "If risk is poorly assessed prior to launching the program." That's not to say going public is bad, it's to understand that being public facing can be risky for an enterprise that isn't ready to take on the inevitable financial and psychological burdens this would involve. It shouldn't come as a surprise that a public program will cost the enterprise much more money than any other program. Visibility equates to greater hacker participation, which converts to vulnerabilities, and in turn the organization is now responsible for paying the security researchers for their work.

An enterprise can easily destroy its reputation in the hacking community if the organization's engineers are not ready to be responsible, or cannot be responsible, for managing too many vulnerabilities. Bug bounty program managers tend to look at programs through rose-tinted glasses. Unfortunately, a jaded perception of application and network strength can result in the destruction of a program that has just barely begun. It's strongly recommended that an enterprise runs a private program for a decent amount of time before taking the leap into the public bug bounty space.

There's not a set requirement for public release, but it's important to know that an organization should never start with a public program. Running a private program for a while gives engineers a chance to understand the bug bounty process, sharpen their skills, and understand the spectrum of vulnerabilities before plunging into a visible world. That's where more participation increases the risk of scrutiny and reputational damage.

3.5.3 Applied Knowledge #3

The hacker takes their SQL vulnerability and searches for a way to report it. Doing a quick search for a security point of contact, the hacker finds a public bug bounty program. Any communicative issues are mitigated and the researcher is able to easily report the vulnerability and be rewarded for their efforts.

When a hacker finds a public program, it's the best possible situation for the researcher to be in. A researcher who can adequately receive a response for their efforts is a researcher who is more likely to be cordial and ready to engage with the enterprise in a constructive manner.

3.5.3.1 Hybrid Models

Mixing multiple models together can easily be the best solution to a complex situation in which a private program is considered too limited and a public program is considered too visible. The standard model is a program that is private in participation, but public-facing. Although private but public-facing sounds confusing, it simply means a program that lets security researchers know they have a program, but it's not actively organized on the bug bounty program platform as a public program that can be participated in. An enterprise can benefit from utilizing a hybrid model as it can help combine the best aspects of bug bounty programs. Even if the program is private, program managers *should implement a security.txt file under the/.well-known/directory of root domains.*

What is a security.txt? (Thanks to Duncan McAlynn @infosecwar for the reminder.)

Simply, it is a means of informing security researchers that a bug bounty program exists. Imagine if a hacker were to poke around at the web application and accidentally stumble upon a vulnerability. They may try to find a security contact at the organization and struggle to do so, which can further complicate the situation. Hackers typically start with fuzzing web applications, and even if the hacker misses the/.well-known/directory while fuzzing, a seasoned researcher is certain to check for a security.txt file manually if they need to report a vulnerability. To understand the best implementation of a security.txt file, please visit: https://securitytxt.org.

3.6 Crowdsourced Platforms

There are multiple bug bounty platform providers to choose from, but it would be a mistake to make a specific recommendation. The key companies that provided bug bounty platform setup and management are Bugcrowd, HackerOne, Integriti, and Synack. Program managers should decide for themselves based on pricing, configuration models, and the other range of functionality options. At the end of the day, application security engineers and their managers need to ensure that a consistent evaluation of their program provider is occurring. Engineers are hired to do a job: build, fix, configure, and innovate – and, as with any other engineering tool, crowdsourcing platforms should be evaluated regularly to enable effective management processes.

The process of identifying an adequate crowdsourcing platform to use is simple: set aside a quarter (roughly three months) to evaluate options. Set aside another quarter in the year to proceed with all of the logistics, a quick proof of concept, and set a date for implementation. Researching and implementing the platform does not include the pre-risk assessments and vulnerability analysis that should occur prior to expanding the enterprise security model. Asking the right questions of platform providers requires a neutral mindset. An application security engineer or general cybersecurity engineer has typically dealt with vendor comparisons. With that being said, there are several suggestions for process improvement, especially when dealing with platform evaluation:

- **Ensure the platform is accredited by hackers as well as engineers:** avoid negative speculation from hackers who haven't been rewarded for bugs to their satisfaction. Research can be conducted on most platforms and by gathering various opinions from engineers and hackers. Additionally, be open minded, as everyone is entitled to their own unique perspective.
- **Without prejudgment, schedule meetings with sales representatives from multiple companies:** if you're working within a strict budget, inform them.
- **Pricing is nearly always an issue, keep in mind that every part of a platform and extended feature is going to accrue an additional cost:** while evaluating platforms, remember that managed triage services, on-demand penetration tests, and bug bounty payouts aren't typically included in standard program deployment.
- **Ask difficult questions, be sure to interject:** remember, if sales representatives have the chance, they will attempt to get through their entire presentation uninterrupted, glossing over the finer details. It's the enterprise's responsibility to evaluate the features being promised and consider what's realistic.
- **Don't offload technical work on a sales representative:** it's not their job to ensure that "x" feature will work with your enterprise model. Instead, formulate an exact question and ask to get in touch with a technical account manager to get a more granular understanding.

On top of the major tips previously mentioned, remember that engineers and management should be in control of the evaluation. Transparency with pricing and features from day one will allow for a more thorough negotiation process. Don't be afraid to tell the vendors you are working with other vendors and looking for the most efficient spending plan.

When vendors are uncontested, you are likely to pay far higher than being transparent in your comparison process.

Overall, any platform will have its advantages and disadvantages, but a good start will be to look for a crowdsourcing vendor that rewards security researchers and fairly mediates issues between programs and researchers. While it may seem advantageous to choose a platform that favors an enterprise's decision on a vulnerability, it's not. Be sure to be on the lookout for solutions that have a bad reputation with the bug bounty hunting community. If researchers avoid the platform, it will not be beneficial for you to use the platform. The last thing an enterprise should want is to receive a poor reputation among the information security community. Program mismanagement can start with a poor platform choice, and the best way to approach a vulnerability disclosure program is starting off with a leg up.

3.7 Platform Pricing and Services

As discussed in Section 3.5, program establishment starts with paying fees for the platform itself. While it is impossible to discuss the granularity of platform pricing, the typical scenario is one in which an enterprise is charged based on its size. A crowdsourcing platform will bridge the gap between security research management and responsible disclosure. A typical deployment involves no infrastructure. Therefore, associated costs will typically be calculated on a standard basis. Comparably, managed services will initiate recurring fees, and on-demand penetration testing services will require fixed-cost fees, depending on services rendered, and so on.

In addition to the recurring annual contracting fees, a program manager must consider the buffer room that must be allocated for a bounty pool. A bounty pool is an allocated amount of money that is committed to paying hackers. Think of it like a prepaid card. An engineer will validate a vulnerability and, if appropriate, triage and assess impact. If the program deems the submission valid, the engineer responsible for managing the vulnerabilities will award the security researcher money, which will be rewarded from the bounty pool.

It's important to note that even though the bounty pool seems simple it usually has associated fees. For example, a platform provider might require that the enterprise pay an "x" percent surcharge to the crowdsourcing platform on top of any bounty. When establishing a bug bounty program, it's important to account for any fees that might occur on top of bounties and any additional services.

3.8 Managed Services

Understanding the necessity for an initial period of managed services requires first knowing what managed services do. Every security research crowdsourcing platform is going to have a different model for the specifics of the services, but at a high level.

Managed services typically include the initial triage of any vulnerabilities that are reported, inviting hackers to the enterprise's program, communicating recommendations and evaluating program analytics, and helping assist in collaboration between the enterprise and the security researcher. Enterprises that are on a budget may opt to avoid purchasing any form of advanced managed services (depending on the platform provider) even from the start, but it's in the best interests of the engineers, or management establishing the program, to use all managed services functionality, at least for a little while. Over time, program managers can downgrade to a model that uses hand-holding techniques less.

Bug bounty programs are not overly complicated, yet many companies fail to effectively manage the workflow and processes that are involved in programs. Managed services can help warm a team up to the various program requirements and best practices before dumping engineers or management into the unknown. As another consideration, most managed service programs will validate vulnerabilities prior to passing them on to the enterprise, helping introduce engineers to new concepts and validation methodologies.

During the establishment of a program, there may be a point in time in which the option to add-on managed services is discussed. There may be a preliminary warm-up period where the platform provider includes these services for free, or it might be an accrued cost from the start, but keep in mind that advanced managed services don't have to be purchased at all or maintained past a given contract period unless otherwise stated.

3.9 Opting Out of Managed Services

Based on experience, the best recommendation would be to never fully opt out of the advanced managed services, unless there's a reason such as poor service or small value from additional managed services add-ons (and depending on the provider, it may not be possible). A reduction from fully managed services to something more partial such as baseline triaging services would be the wisest move with time.

Advanced managed services is a best practice to ensure that the program receives analytics and feedback to progress, which isn't usually provided in a standard baseline model. Noting that it's a best practice and not a requirement is an important difference because the enterprise setting up a program may be able to completely validate, triage, and remediate vulnerabilities without any third-party involvement. If the organization setting up the program has the capacity to reduce the provided options and move to a baseline level of managed services without negatively impacting reputation or tarnishing a security researcher's work, by all means, use best judgment.

In addition, it's not usually possible to fully opt out of managed services. If a program manager had the ability to do so, they could neglect a program.

3.10 On-demand Penetration Tests

Many security research crowdsourcing platforms offer on-demand penetration tests. The penetration tests offered by these platforms are similar to traditional testing methodology in the sense that there are typically findings that are presented and remediation methodology. The best way to think of crowdsourced penetration testers are as expert bug bounty hunters. The researchers assigned to the penetration test will likely find a decent amount of client and server side exploits.

There's no question that one might wonder about the efficiency of purchasing an application penetration test. In terms of compliance, there isn't adequate evidence to believe that purchasing a dedicated test is any more efficient than running a program. A bug bounty program is an ongoing incentive: the enterprise running this program is consistently being tested on. However, the program itself cannot fulfill the compliance requirements for penetration testing criteria as it's impossible to have full oversight being tested by the researchers participating in your program. Instead, hire a third-party penetration testing company and put applications in scope for testing. An enterprise can bundle together the network and application assets to maximize the money spent on testing, especially if the budget is particularly tight.

Overall, an application penetration test offered through a crowdsourcing program isn't necessarily required. As a note, if the enterprise has enough money to perform a wide array of testing, it wouldn't hurt to purchase the services. Before the services are purchased, ensure that the bug bounty program is ready to be tested on. In order to determine readiness, the program should be actively receiving bugs for at least a year and have had some major vulnerabilities reported. It wouldn't be recommended to start this testing until the program is major enough to timely resolve any reported bugs. If a junior program uses a penetration testing service as described, it could end up being a waste of money – especially if the software development lifecycle isn't using the best possible application security processes. As described previously, if the objective is to establish a thorough and respectable program, it wouldn't make much sense to throw an enterprise into an arena that the program isn't currently prepared for.

Part 3

Program Setup

4

Defining Program Scope and Bounties

4.1   What Is a Bounty?

Simply put, a bounty is a reward paid to a security researcher. Bounty programs establish a way for a researcher to disclose bugs of impact to organizations. The enterprise has the ability to define various reward tiers to encourage participation.

Bounties should never be viewed as paying for exploitation, but for adequate and detailed vulnerability research.

4.2   Understanding Scope

Scope can be a confusing topic for some engineers. Historically, scope has been a means of defining what researchers are allowed to target. Scope can be tricky in the sense that anything not defined as "out of scope" can be fair game to a researcher. When engineers imagine "fair game," they may envision assets, yet, realistically it can also pertain to methodology used by security researchers. Imagine this: a researcher finds a program, and there's nothing in the out-of-scope definitions that state brute force attacks (i.e. attempts to submit many passwords or passphrases in the hope of eventually guessing the correct combination) as being out of scope. A researcher now has unlimited time to run through enumerated usernames and test for account takeover. As a secondary consideration, they may negatively impact the application. The researcher spends a couple of days attempting "credential stuffing" against an application login portal and now gains unauthenticated access to an account. The enterprise must now pay this attacker for a high or critical payout depending on the program definitions. It's qualified as a full account takeover.

A scenario such as the one provided above could have been completely avoided if the engineer setting up the program understood the applications, attack methodologies, and so on.

Corporate Cybersecurity: Identifying Risks and the Bug Bounty Program, First Edition. John Jackson.
© 2021 John Wiley & Sons, Ltd. Published 2021 by John Wiley & Sons, Ltd.

4.3 How to Create Scope

Many engineers approach scope with the idea of limiting the attack surface for a researcher. Limiting the attack surface for a researcher is absurd, and the complete reverse methodology that should be used for increasing the security of enterprise application development. Instead, a better approach is to start with a smaller amount of assets and work up to a larger attack surface when reports start to dwindle.

For example, compare two models of scope and notice subtle changes to the web testing portion of the scope.

4.3.1 Models

Model A (1st Month of Program Setup):
In-Scope
Web:

1. https://example.com/login
2. https://example.com/policies
3. https://example.com/legal
4. https://dev.example.com/about-us
5. https://dev.example.com/login
6. https://dev.example.com/profile
7. https://dev.example.com/customer/support-services

Model B (6th Month of Program Setup):
In-Scope
Web:

1. https://example.com*
2. https://dev.example.com*
3. https://staging.example.com/join
4. https://staging.example.com/about-us
5. https://testing.example.com

While comparing both models A and B, it's easy to see that staging and testing were added to the web scope (subdomains), but why are fewer assets listed overall? Both the example.com and the dev.example.com subdomains now have wildcards. It's standard to eventually use wildcards where possible.

4.4 Understanding Wildcards

Wildcards are fairly simple to understand. They are a means of allowing for a wider attacker surface. A wildcard can help a program identify more vulnerabilities, and give a security researcher more flexibility to stick to an enterprise's program and get to know it and want to test on the program. One of the biggest complaints that researchers will touch on is the lack of wildcards in a program. Some researchers will not participate in any programs that don't use wildcards because they don't have the breadth that a researcher is looking for.

When thinking about wildcards, there are several methodologies:

- Subdomain: *.example.com
- Domain: example.com/*
- Specific Domain Path: example.com/login/*
- Subdomain Path: dev.example.com/*

4.4.1   Subdomain

Simply, a program that sets a wildcard domain is using the most permissive scenario possible. Imagine, for instance, that example.com has subdomains such as mail.example.com, app.example.com, dev.example.com, etc.; a security researcher can test any of these subdomains, on any URL path. An important consideration to be made before allowing a wildcard in the subdomain slot of a domain is whether the engineers who are managing the program have done their due diligence and evaluated all of the subdomains or not. It would be a poor decision to allow a subdomain wildcard if the full attack surface weren't evaluated.

Example

A security researcher finds a login portal for a service on one of the subdomains. The subdomain is configured poorly and the researcher manages to exploit the application and get employee login credentials, but the application portal has nothing of value. Knowing that employees are likely to reuse credentials, the researcher then finds another subdomain that is an Admin management portal for all of the web application code, and the researcher logins to the application, and has full access to modify, deploy, or delete any of the production website's code.

Does this example seem unrealistic? It can and has happened. An engineer has to ensure that the subdomains in scope are being evaluated just as the main domain of the web application is. There are a plethora of attacks that can impact subdomain and turn critical if unchecked.

4.4.2   Domain

Wildcard use on domains is typically the in-between scope option for bug bounty programs. A researcher who tests against a basic domain wildcard can perform research on the entire domain, but any identified subdomains would not be in scope unless otherwise stated. As explained earlier, it would not be advisable to use a domain or subdomain wildcard without knowing all paths or assets that could be tested.

4.4.3   Specific Domain Path or Specific Subdomain Path

Unless there's a wide range of URLs involved, a specific path asset set as in scope typically maintains the least permissive testing posture. Programs that are just being established can get the feel for bug bounty programs by using this model and setting certain domain paths as in scope. The more critical paths, such as /login or/checkout, are a necessity to test against because malicious hackers will attempt to exploit any low-hanging fruit that may be exposed on these paths.

4.5   Determining Asset Allocation

Enterprise bug bounty programs will typically have a vastly different setup, depending on the specific field that the company actively participates in. For example, a medical company may be concerned with protecting patient records, and may use a model that allows doctors or nurses to log in to a web portal that allows them to access patient records. What company in its right mind would allow such a critical asset to be exposed to the public? Well, the reality is, if it's absolutely necessary to expose critical assets to the public, they need to be checked. Paying a couple thousand dollars to a security researcher is nowhere near the level of pain that will occur if vital information were to leak to the public.

To a medical organization, protecting patient records is vital. Just ask Alberto Hill, who on a dark day performed security research, logging into a public facing web portal with the username "admin" and the password "admin." All legal issues aside, Alberto had access to financial records, medical records, medication information, and so on. Alberto's story can teach engineers that putting the most critical assets in scope for a bug bounty program isn't optional: it's a requirement. If the engineers managing the program are not ready to allow researchers to test these assets, the first part of the journey is understood: the engineers know that it's important to assess these assets and should adequately do so, in some form.

One size can never fit all for an organization identifying assets. As another example, consider an ecommerce website that focuses on selling digital assets. Some of the biggest risks that a digital sales website could face are account takeover opportunities, stealing assets through business logic, or insecure web application code, and so on. Depending on the model of the enterprise, there may be less of a risk for exposed customer data, and more of a risk of theft or manipulation. The best possible thing an engineer can do while setting up a program is to consider the logic of their critical company assets, test them, and put parts or entire domains, subdomains, etc. in scope.

Web applications are just the tip of the iceberg for bug bounty programs. Crowdsourcing platforms have been known to allow enterprises to include mobile applications and public-facing network assets in their program testing scope. Some of the bigger companies have even made the news for coordinating with their top hackers and sending the latest hardware or tech for testing purposes, allowing researchers to keep the hardware when testing is complete.

Overall, whoever is tasked with establishing the bug bounty program will have to consider what assets to put into scope. Only the engineers establishing the program can make this determination. The recommended release order would depend on whether the company manufactured physical goods. For example, if the company in question were an Internet service provider, it would make sense to allow security researchers to test their own home routers if the company produced those routers. Obviously, the stipulation would be that a researcher refrained from damaging the hardware, or less they will have to pay for it.

An application security engineer running a program, for instance, can collaborate with network security, infrastructure, mobile teams, and so on, to determine important assets to test. The best way to view asset allocation is with the mindset that one can always expand, but it's harder to retract. If an enterprise puts all wildcards for subdomains and every main domain in scope and has 100 vulnerabilities reported within the first 24 hours, these assets can be pulled out of scope. But the researcher's findings will stand and have to be addressed according to the service level agreement (SLA) guidelines that are defined in the program. An SLA is a commitment between a service provider and a client. In this instance, the bug bounty program sets an SLA and the researchers agree to their promise to address or patch vulnerabilities in the appropriate timeframe.

4.6 Asset Risk

Outside of determining what assets are appropriate for the scope of the program, it's essential to understand production impact. While it's typically a good idea to put critical assets in scope, bug bounty program managers must ask: "Why is this critical?" If it's critical because of sensitive information, that's one scenario. However, if it's critical because testing can cause major impact or financial loss, it should not be put into the scope unless the program is certain that it will not cause major issues.

While it's difficult to evaluate every possible scenario in which there can be impact for production components, engineers must try to identify any conflicts where possible. In the event that impact does occur, communicate the notion quickly to software engineers and be transparent about the situation. Hiding facts will not help remediate any issues that may occur, and taking ownership is the best possible solution.

4.7 Understanding Out of Scope

While it may seem ridiculous to describe the meaning of "out of scope," there's more to the equation than just defining assets that are not "in scope." It can take a careful hand to appropriately decide what assets shouldn't be tested on, and out of scope represents more than just what *shouldn't* be tested on. Initiating the most thorough program requires knowing the type of attacks that are out there and creating a scope that prevents disruption.

First and foremost, as a baseline, it's important to assign testing environments and assets that you don't want a research to test to the out-of-scope section. In most instances forgetting to include certain assets in your out-of-scope section isn't detrimental. Security researchers should know to avoid testing on anything that isn't defined as "in scope," and they undoubtedly want to get paid. Don't inadvertently assume that all security researchers will respect the rules of the bug bounty program. In many instances, security researchers will test on whatever they feel like in hopes they can abuse it to prove that it's in scope. Additionally, researchers may ignore specific prohibited testing criteria by proxy-chaining (the act of changing IP address with each new request), and engineers managing the bug bounty program must keep this in mind.

When considering what to prohibit, it's recommended to put the majority of the most common disruptive techniques in the out-of-scope section; this is a formality. Prohibiting disruptive behavior is a formality because, as stated, it will not stop anyone from performing those actions. As the program manager, don't punish security researchers for their testing methodologies. At the end of the day if there isn't disruption it's not problematic. It's the old adage: don't make mountains out of molehills.

As a general rule of thumb, here's a pocket guide to some of the major vulnerabilities and testing methodology that should be included in the out-of-scope section, along with the "why."

4.8 Vulnerability Types

4.8.1 Denial of Service (DOS) or Distributed Denial of Service (DDoS) Attacks

In short, DOS or DDoS attacks can cause production impact and take servers down that host major services. Even if the security researcher doesn't test it, but presents possible DOS or DDoS attacks on "x" server or service, there are minimal cases in which this finding is worth anything.

4.8.2 Social Engineering Attacks

Many subtechniques within the category of social engineering are exceedingly effective. However, save the testing of these techniques for hired penetration testers. It's generally not a good idea to include social engineering attacks as in scope, because this could cause potential legal issues if an employee or customer ends up having any sensitive data leaked.

In addition to legal liability, social engineering attacks can be disruptive to enterprise workflow. A constant barrage of phishing emails via contact forms, emails, phone calls (or whatever the means may be) can result in employee complaints or cause monetary loss depending on the specific instance. It's important to be adamant about excluding social engineering attacks due to the possibility of disruption.

4.8.3 Brute Force or Rate Limiting

Attacks that include attempting to break into user accounts (brute force) can possibly cause issues as well. Brute force attacks can disrupt the application security workflow and also cause legal issues if user accounts are taken over and abused in the security research "proof of concept" process. In addition to legal issues, brute force attacks can negatively affect production environments, and in the instance it goes down, the application security team may be responsible for not annotating this as out of scope.

Rate limiting should also be included as out of scope for the same reasons. Security researchers may disrupt production environments and cause impact or other related security issues. In addition, it's considerably low impact.

4.8.4 Account and Email Enumeration

Building a list of usernames or emails that exist on the application typically has no impact on the enterprise. In this day and age of technology, it's become exceedingly easy to gather wordlists of usernames and emails to use for brute force attacks.

4.8.5 Self-XSS

Being able to produce an XSS (cross-site scripting) alert that can only be seen by the user themselves and not anyone else, including staff, is not generally considered a vulnerability. Self-XSS has no considerable impact. However, program managers must understand the difference between all of the various XSS types to ensure that they understand the security researcher.

4.8.6 Clickjacking

Clickjacking is the practice of manipulating a user's activity by concealing hyperlinks beneath legitimate clickable content, thereby causing the user to perform actions of which they are unaware. Clickjacking is also known as a "UI redress attack". The vulnerability of clickjacking is usually out of scope because it relies on social engineering heavily. It can be used to exploit users, but generally not in the scope of vulnerabilities that a program should/would accept.

4.8.7 Miscellaneous

Realistically, there are far too many attacks that can be considered nonpayable. Program managers should take the time to review all of the various attack methods and look at other attacks that are out of scope in similar bug bounty programs to determine why allowing that type of attack may end up being problematic. Keep in mind that expansions are continuous. Program managers will find that certain types of attacks may be too disruptive to their workflow or considerably low impact and not worth evaluating. Assess the out-of-scope attack vector portion of programs as needed, and be sure to inform hackers of any major modifications.

4.9 When Is an Asset Really Out of Scope?

Overall, the objective of out-of-scope reporting is never to discourage a security researcher from reporting, but to ensure that baseline restrictions are placed to prevent legal or financial impact. With that being considered, ideally program managers should be fair in the evaluation of vulnerabilities that are in and out of scope.

A security researcher pulls up a list subdomains for the enterprise and finds a lot of assets, some of which are explicitly stated as out of scope. Researchers are curious, be it by nature or acquired in their lives. They want to know how components work. In this specific scenario, assume that it's well known that this asset is out of scope (defined in the out-of-scope section of the enterprise bug bounty program): should it be tested on?

If the answer that came to mind was *no*, it can be simultaneously the right and wrong answer. To demonstrate scenarios that bug bounty program managers may run into, consider an example of a (P1) – critical vulnerability – and a (P4) – low vulnerability.

(P1) – Critical: Admin Account Takeover

In this scenario, while testing on various subdomains, the researcher notices something strange. It appears that one of the subdomains that was found was "admin.prod.example.com." The researcher reviews the scope and sees that *.prod.example.com is listed as out of scope. Nonetheless, curiosity takes over, and to the researcher's surprise, they find an exposed client side Laravel Debugbar. At this point, they have to make a choice, "To go out of scope or not?"

Now, in the case of the Laravel Debugbar, imagine that the researcher intercepts admin credentials and is able to log in to the web application that resides on the admin endpoint. The web application portal has internal employee email addresses, sensitive workflow information, client addresses and other contact information, and so on. A moral dilemma occurs and the researcher now has to decide if it's worth it to even report a vulnerability that is identified as "out of scope."

In most circumstances, the researcher will report the vulnerability, especially if it pertains to account takeover or PII (personally identifiable information).

Now, review the next scenario, keeping the P1 example in mind.

(P4) – Low: Apache Server Status Page Leaking Server Information

Comparably, the same security researcher may have stumbled upon a subdomain named "sv1.prod.example.com." As our previous example stated, *.prod.example.com is out of scope. When loading the web page, the researcher finds the/server-status page of the webserver and can now see specific information, such as versioning, URL paths that it records, CPU usage, and some internal IP addresses.

While this may seem like a serious vulnerability to an amateur researcher, the severity of such vulnerability completely depends on the level of information that can be accessed. For example, if this server-status page records all root domain endpoints, it's possible that the researcher will find an endpoint that reveals sensitive information after navigating to it. However, if no sensitive information is revealed, whether outright or through recorded endpoints, the vulnerability will be treated as a low.

The researcher once again will have to make a choice, to report it or not. In many instances it may just be reported out of love for doing the right thing. The researcher knows they are in the hands of a program manager to decide if they are going to get paid or not. Nonetheless, a bug bounty program manager will have to make the right decision on paying the hacker. Alternatively, with the utilization of bug bounty platform providers, program managers can resolve the report with no monetary awards that can still be beneficial to the researcher's credibility.

4.10 The House Wins – Or Does It?

The ultimate decision of many bug bounty programs that currently operate typically resides with not paying the security researcher if it's out of scope. Some that have been overheard reside within the school of thought of "We don't want to encourage our researchers to hack out-of-scope assets just to get a bounty" or "If we pay a researcher for one out-of-scope bounty, we will have to pay them for every out-of-scope bounty."

A major issue with adverse thinking toward out-of-scope research is that it can lead to key research being overlooked. When determining whether paying for a reported vulnerability appears to be the right move, ask the following questions:

1. What is the level of impact of this vulnerability? Could it lead to extremely sensitive information leakage?
2. If no sensitive information is leaked, could the vulnerability severely damage company reputation?
3. Do we value the researcher and want to reward them?

One size does not fit all in terms of paying a security researcher. Remember, when managing a program, the rules are made by the program manager. While transparency with leadership must always be exercised, caring is the key to developing a strong and loyal research platform and building brand reputation among the cybersecurity community. Let's take our earlier examples of the critical and low vulnerabilities and perform a dry run of answering the above questions.

P1 – Admin Account Takeover

1. What is the level of impact of this vulnerability? Could it lead to extremely sensitive information leakage? Yes, the researcher has found multiple pieces of PII and information that can be valuable if sold to or obtained by a threat actor.
2. If no sensitive information is leaked, could the vulnerability severely damage company reputation? Even if the researcher could not leak sensitive information, this admin panel contains functionality that could take down key parts of the business, resulting in monetary impact, in turn resulting in reputational damage.
3. Do we value the researcher and want to reward them? Personally, this researcher has never reported to us before, but it would be nice to reward them for their efforts.

In this admin takeover example, it's easily determined that a lot of damage could occur. Company information could be sold, or there could be direct impact to business continuity, creating a loss in revenue. With that being said, the right thing to do would be to pay the security researcher. In a circumstance such as the one described, there would be far more loss in a breach scenario than there would ever be if the researcher were adequately paid. Programs should consider setting a moral example and paying for the vulnerability findings.

P4 – Apache Server Status Page Leaking Server Information

1. What is the level of impact of this vulnerability? Could it lead to extremely sensitive information leakage? No, there's no sensitive information leakage. Several internal IPs are displayed, but no impact.
2. If no sensitive information is leaked, could the vulnerability severely damage company reputation? No, there's no reputational damage.
3. Do we value the researcher and want to reward them? This researcher has reported to us many times before. However, we don't see any severe impact.

When a lower-end vulnerability is reported out of scope, it's not technically immoral to refuse to reward hackers for their findings. Expectations that were set out early in the process are fair game. However, consider paying researchers a mild bonus or sending a t-shirt. A little bit of gratitude, especially for someone who went out of their way to help, goes a long way.

4.11 Fair Judgment on Bounties

It's easy to stray from the moral path as a program manager. At times, it can seem enticing to claim plausible deniability for an issue. If using a managed program, the triagers only know your environment as well as they possibly can from an external perspective. Bug bounty programs are only as efficient as the engineers and managers that run the program. Similarly, programs can only be as honest as the parties responsible for validating vulnerabilities.

There are many blind exploitation paths that can easily be denied, or are questionable from the perspective of an attacker, and it takes adequate communication between the researcher and engineer to confirm the existence of some vulnerabilities.

If a researcher were to stumble across a GitHub repository for an organization and find SQL credentials, it would be an extremely valuable finding, especially if they could log in. In the instance that the login is restricted to the internal network, they may not have a way to immediately control the server. At times, it may take internal verification. Verification may fall out of the line of sight of the triage team and the researcher.

Observe the following interaction between a triage team, program, and hacker.

Part 1: Security Researcher to Triage

Security researcher: Hello, I found a vulnerability. It appears that a live production server that the company owns has accidentally committed cleartext SQL server credentials to the public GitHub repository. Unfortunately, login was not possible as it was noted that the SQL server restricts logins to the internal network. A precise pivot point wasn't identified. Therefore, I decided to just go ahead and report it to get the credentials out of rotation.

<Impact Statement>
<Writeup>
<Credentials>

Triage: Thank you for your report! We will get back to you after further validation with the team.

Part 2: Triage to Program

Triage: I have reviewed the researcher's report, and more information is needed. Unfortunately, I was unable to verify if the credentials are legitimately in use in the production environment due to internal subnet restrictions. Can you please validate?

Program: Sure, we will check to see if the credentials are still in use.
24 hours later

Program: Hi. We've contacted the infrastructure team responsible for maintaining the server. They have validated that the credentials are no longer in use.

Triage: Thank you for the information. I will let the researcher know.

Part 3: Triage to Researcher (Response to Part 2)

Triage: After discussion with the program, it was determined that these credentials are not in use. I am sorry to report that this will be closed out as an informational vulnerability. We encourage you to continue your research and submit any relevant reports.

Report closed

4.12 Post-mortem

When reviewing the reporting process, it's seemingly harmless, right? The researcher submits what they believe to be a vulnerability, and the enterprise confirms that the credentials are no longer in use. What if they *were* in use? Would the triagers or security researcher know the difference? The unfortunate answer is a simple, *no*. Unless the researcher has adequate proof that they were able to interact with the server, not much can be done at this point. Nothing is stopping the application security team from inquiring with the team maintaining the credentials, who then decide to rotate the credentials and pretend that the vulnerability never existed.

The situation in which a program steals vulnerability findings from a security researcher isn't unrealistic. In fact, many security researchers can attest to the theft of such research. The issue with a bug bounty program versus a security researcher is that of monetary and legal binding. A large enterprise typically has lawyers on hand who can contribute toward the cause in the event of legal fallout. In addition, programs use blanket nondisclosure agreements (NDAs) to bind researchers into silence. While the intention of most programs isn't to use an NDA as a means of trapping researchers into legal battles and stealing research, *it has happened*. Determining fault is yet another tricky situation. The program manager responding to the incident may not have checked to see if the credentials were working, or may not have been able to because of enterprise restrictions. Communication is essential to the mitigation of further issues during these circumstances.

4.13 Awareness and Reputational Damage

The intent of highlighting the issues that some security researchers will face isn't to shame programs. As an engineer or manager working on or running a program the takeaway is to realize that technical ineptitude or immoral behavior isn't excusable. Professionals need to do their part to contribute to the greater good, and in the scenarios in which vulnerability research is stolen, or payment is blatantly refused, it can directly impact the enterprise.

Social media is the new norm. Most businesses maintain social media pages, and it's not uncommon to witness upper management frequently using popular social media websites. An unintended consequence of running a bug bounty program poorly is escalation from security researchers on social media websites. When a researcher does not feel heard, or they determine that their research is being stolen, don't be surprised to see them take to social media with their concerns. An NDA via participating in a bug bounty platform seems like an effective countermeasure. However, it's rarely the be all and end all from a researcher. Many people have no issue or second thought about getting their bug hunting profile banned if it means that they have the ability to possibly hold program managers to account.

Bug bounty hunting is a niche trade. There are not millions of bug bounty hunters getting paid for their research. With that being said, the community is small enough to develop an internal burn list of programs that have been notably sketchy in their communications or resolution. Ask any seasoned bug bounty hunter which programs should be avoided and they will more than likely have a list of programs to avoid like the plague. Researchers aren't always being wronged. The unfortunate truth resides in the fact that sometimes the captain goes down with the ship – or in other words, even if a security researcher is in the wrong, they may possibly fight the program, and cause great reputational harm.

4.14   Putting It All Together

The moral of the story: running a program requires patience, and honesty. At times, the level of truthfulness that is required is deafening, and can feel self-defeating. No one program manager or engineer working on a program has all of the answers. It's not unreasonable to assume that a situation may occur in which a vulnerability is difficult to understand, or seems downright impossible to grasp. In situations where comprehension of a vulnerability is lacking, reach out to other individuals in the application security space and ask for guidance.

It does not hurt to get a second opinion on a report, and individuals working in the cybersecurity space need to know when it's appropriate to do so. Everyone wants to be a superstar, but being an application security expert requires knowing when to ask for help and when to work through the issue alone. Researchers are not obligated to work with enterprises. A lot of the vulnerabilities identified through bug bounty programs can be abused for financial exploitation far past any monetary amount that the company would have paid for the vulnerability.

4.15   Bug Bounty Payments

While there are many ways to determine responsible payout amounts, the realism lies with the program type, enterprise budget, and visibility of the program. Payments can never be a one-size-fits-all scenario, so it's important to keep that in mind when determining the right payment table. There are several questions and steps that can be taken to assist in the determination process and make it enjoyable for both the program and security researcher.

4.15.1 Determining Payments

First and foremost, before anything pertaining to payments is created, know this: can a monetary amount be assigned to the value of vulnerability mitigation? Running a bug bounty program means that a monetary value *has* to be assigned, or at least some form of compensation. However, remember that a breach can be far more painful and costly than any form of payment that would be given to a security researcher. In the instance where a program pays $10,000 for a critical vulnerability, that could be a drop in the bucket compared to millions of dollars that could be paid in the instance of threat actor exploitation.

With payment amounts in mind, there are two options: set values or set ranges. While setting specific reward values may seem like a great option, it limits the scope and ability to determine granularity, especially in the instance that a vulnerability is riding a fine line between a high and a critical rating, or a medium and a low rating. Program reward ranges per vulnerability criticality is an incredibly useful option for tricky situations.

A security researcher discovers a stored XSS vulnerability. Unfortunately, it's a payload that can only be stored in a part of the application that is exceedingly limited in scope. Maybe it requires an expensive subscription in which the realism of replicating the attack against another user becomes fairly unlikely. Nonetheless, there's a potential in which this attack may be considered "low paying," or not qualified for payment at all. Now, imagine that the researcher reports it, and during the reporting process the engineer triaging the vulnerability triggers the stored-XSS vulnerability, and it results in an authentication token for a separate internal user management platform being acquired. A scenario described as such isn't unlikely, and has happened to other companies in the past.

Bug bounty program managers have now successfully evaluated the bug, and it appears to be a self-XSS vulnerability. The engineer managing the program marks this vulnerability as out of scope. After the report is marked as disqualifying, the researcher takes note of the logging mechanism attached to the domain that was used in their XSS payload, and notices the token. The researcher has now successfully obtained access to the enterprise user management portal. Inside of the company portal, there are thousands of pieces of personally identifiable information and unlimited access to perform account actions on other users.

In a scenario described as the one above, the security researcher has taken an action that may have been considered out of scope or a low-payable action, and has completely escalated it to a critical vulnerability. As a program manager, it has to be decided how to pay the researcher – if at all. However, the situation has escalated into a bit of a predicament. Should the program pay the researcher?

Earlier in the chapter, it is stated that critical research is valuable. However, the actions were resultant of a specific scenario that may be considered out of scope from several different angles (social engineering, nearly self-XSS). When a situation occurs in which you want to pay a researcher, but maybe not as much, a rewards range can make the difference.

The difference between the values and the range make quite the impact (see Table 4.1). In the described situation in which a researcher performs the stored XSS abuse (which may be considered somewhat out of scope), a program that wants to compensate the researcher fairly might struggle. They most certainly don't want to pay them $5000 but, on the other hand, paying $3000 isn't quite on the cards, based on the out-of-scope effort and the level of complexity required in exploitation.

Table 4.1 Setting Bug Bounty Reward Values and Ranges.

Set Reward Values			
Critical	High	Medium	Low
$5000	$3000	$1000	$200
Set Reward Range			
Critical	High	Medium	Low
$3500–$5000	$1500–$3000	$400–$1000	$50–$200

A reward range makes more sense. The program knows that they don't want to pay the researcher between $3500 and $5000, and $3000 was undoubtedly a little too steep for the specific scenario. Luckily, the range varies between $1500 and $3000. The program then decides to pay the researcher $1500 dollars. Reward ranges give an enterprise breathing room when more complicated vulnerability submission events occur. Instead of paying a hefty $3000 for an event that was out of scope, a program can now choose to pay $1500 – rewarding the researcher for their efforts (without discounting the research) and maintaining a positive affirmation for researchers that stay in scope by giving them the potential to earn $3000.

4.15.2 Bonus Payments

The burning question: "When should a bonus payment be used?"

A bonus payment should be used in instances where there's a unique circumstance. For example, if a researcher were to find a duplicate vulnerability but write a highly extensive report detailing the vulnerability in length and provide new evidence, consider a bonus payment. Bonus payments don't have to be excessive or used frequently, but they can be a way to say thanks to an awesome researcher.

An alternate use case for bonus payments is when exploitation bypasses the normal means of criticality, and the bug bounty program wants to be fair. Imagine a program in which the top reward (critical) was set at $4500. In an instance where a researcher was able to pivot from the web application to the backend, and from the backend server to the domain controller and obtain sensitive information, would $4500 be a fair reward? Bonus payments can help extend enterprise reward capacity without requiring an extremely large reward range to be set by the program manager. There's not a set answer when it comes to awarding researchers bonus payments. Use the best possible discretion and be willing to reward researchers for creative instances of vulnerability exploitation.

4.15.3 Nonmonetary Rewards

An aspect that's frequently overlooked in the payment process is "swag." A lot of programs can benefit by using swag as a motivating incentive. It shouldn't come as a surprise that many security researchers like to hack because it's fun. In fact, most CVEs (common vulnerabilities and exposures) are a result of security researchers putting in their hard-earned time to submit research for free. Swag as it applies to bug bounty programs should be something unique that cannot be bought from the enterprise apparel shop with money – think "feat of strength" or "unique."

There are many instances in which swag can be used as a way to bolster program strength, or to encourage security researchers to participate. Some of the more commonly used methods are:

1. Researcher finds an exceedingly critical bug.
2. Researchers who frequently participate in or have contributed a lot of research to a program.
3. As an alternate payment for vulnerabilities that are rated as "low."
4. As an alternate payment for vulnerabilities that are rated as "informational" but provide important perspectives that may not have been known otherwise.
5. Used as an incentive to hack during a certain timeframe or for a specific vulnerability type ("Find a way to buy items from our store for free and we will reward researchers with payment + special swag").

At times, swag is avoided because enterprises worry about budgetary restrictions. After all, many program managers may not want to have to buy 50 or more t-shirts or hoodies as a minimum print requirement. Therefore, a program manager should consider a print-on-demand service. A quick search will bring up many options for print on demand. It's a service that boasts flexibility to be able to fully customize products with a design provided by the user, and there's typically no minimum order fulfillment requirements. Creativity integrated in a modest way with bug bounty programs can help the program stand out. Security researchers will likely post about the uniqueness and creativity of the program online (plus it's free marketing).

The one disclaimer with swag is to minimize using it in instances where the program being managed is in the private stage, or has no intentions of being in the public space. Security researchers are relentless in their desires. They may hack the company solely for obtaining a piece of apparel or an item, and this could be problematic if the program is private, causing resentment. As ridiculous as that sounds, considering all of the possibilities of a researcher's mindset contributes directly to the success of a program. Ideally, if a program manager runs a private program and wants to give out swag, kindly instruct the researcher not to post pictures of the swag on social media. (But please consider if the researcher decides to ignore the request to perform automated scans anyway, as this may occur.)

5

Understanding Safe Harbor and Service Level Agreements

5.1 What Is "Safe Harbor"?

Safe harbor is the means of a bug bounty program providing affirmation to a researcher whom they will not seek legal action against the researcher if the researcher is acting in good faith within the constraints of the program scope and rules.

5.1.1 The Reality of Safe Harbor

Program managers may feel a bit out of place while writing a safe harbor agreement. Safe harbors contain legal jargon and can seem intimidating, especially when it's the program's responsibility to at least work up a simple safe harbor clause. It's important to note that this isn't always the case. Most modern-day bug bounty platforms allow a program manager to use a templated safe harbor agreement, and in all actuality that's all a safe harbor is: a templated nonaction clause.

5.1.2 Fear and Reluctance

Most security researchers are willing to poke around an enterprise's assets, regardless of whether the asset is in scope or not (or if they even have a program). Nonetheless, that cannot be said of every researcher. Security researchers have different flavors of hacking, and for some that means acting only in the most legitimate sense of ethics. Program managers need to heed the safe harbor recommendation. Not every bug bounty program has a full safe harbor plan, and in many cases there isn't one at all.

It's not recommended to operate a bug bounty program without a safe harbor plan. A safe harbor can actually work in the benefit of a program and researcher. When security researchers want to be protected, they will look for the safe harbor clause, and synonymously programs can use it to protect themselves in a court of law if research goes awry.

Corporate Cybersecurity: Identifying Risks and the Bug Bounty Program, First Edition. John Jackson.
© 2021 John Wiley & Sons, Ltd. Published 2021 by John Wiley & Sons, Ltd.

5.1.3 Writing Safe Harbor Agreements

First and foremost, it may be unnecessary to write a handcrafted safe harbor clause. As stated previously, many bug bounty platforms give the program manager an option to fully integrate a templated safe harbor agreement that would hold up in a court of law. In the instance a safe harbor needs to be written, it's likely because the enterprise is running its own program without using a bug bounty platform.

Here are some tips for writing an effective safe harbor agreement:

- Let the researcher know they are expected to respect any hacking laws that may be relevant in their country or region.
- Ensure that they understand the research must be conducted in good faith and that, as long as it's done in such manner, they are exempt from legal action and free to conduct research.
- Repeat that the enterprise will not take any negative legal action against them if assets that are considered in scope are exploited.
- Communicate that accidental violations of the policy which were not intended to be malicious are forgiven.
- Provide means of contact in the event that the researcher has any questions about the safe harbor agreement.

5.1.4 Example Safe Harbor Agreement

Safe Harbor

Please review the follow agreement before testing:

- You are expected to always know the laws of security research as they apply to your country or region. We are not responsible for any violations of specific guidelines set out by your area of residence.
- Research must be conducted in good faith. Doing so exempts the researcher from legal action and allows the researcher to test against our services.
- Legal action will not be taken against any individuals exploiting services or assets considered "in scope."
- Accidental violations of the safe harbor policies set forward may be qualified as long as the research conducted was done so in good faith.

In the event that you have questions or concerns about the safe harbor agreement, please contact us at: example@testing.com.

Generally speaking, the above safe harbor agreement represents a good start – although, again, it's recommended that the program managers use anything templated by bug bounty platforms or consult with lawyers when drawing up custom safe harbor agreements.

5.2 Retaliation against a Rogue Researcher (Cybercriminal or Threat/Bad Actor)

It's not always easy to make a determination of criminal activity versus criminal activity. In a sense, exploitation that may have sounded all of the alarms in the past can turn into a daily, weekly, or monthly occurrence. Before starting a program, knowing what your usual attack patterns look like is essential to be able to separate legitimate individuals from malicious ones. Typically, attack patterns can be analyzed via SIEM (security information and event management) logs or the web application security firewall, and hopefully at this point a program has not been established without these key tools. Identifying legitimate attacks versus pseudo-attacks becomes second nature after working on a program for a little bit of time – but deciding when to prosecute is a different story.

The unfortunate part of working in the cybersecurity field is that we may not necessarily maintain the ability to prosecute anyone who's deemed a threat actor. Getting legal assistance depends on the structure of the organization and the type of attack that has occurred. Every situation may vary, and it will be up to the program managers to attempt to figure out the behavior patterns of a threat actor.

For example, a program manager may have had a negative communication with a researcher pertaining to a vulnerability that was considered social engineering, and therefore out of scope. If the researcher decides they are going to turn into a threat actor, all cards are up in the air. The beauty of a bug bounty program is that a situation like this provides a good paper trail of evidence in the event that this actor decides they want to go rogue. However, in a situation where the vulnerability was leaked on the dark web or it was sourced through someone else, it may be harder to determine the course of action.

Generally speaking, one of the best things that can be done when the program is feeling threatened by the research is to gather logistical evidence that the researcher has gone rogue with their vulnerability. This may include logs, screenshots, the report from the bug bounty platform, and proof of exploitation. A transparent chain of custody may help expedite the legal process to legal and hopefully bring any threats to an actionable state. However, realize that, as a program manager, you should be vigilant but not looking to punish researchers. Exercise caution, but don't look for ways to punish legitimate researchers. One wrong move in which a security researcher is confused as a threat actor could ruin company reputation.

Another risk may be the possibility of the researcher leaking the vulnerability through social media or other public channels. In an instance like this, a program manager should proceed with caution to avoid a witch hunt. A researcher may not always be in the right, and even in an instance of a legitimate vulnerability, community retaliation can be deadly and attempts to mask the vulnerability can result in the Streisand effect. (The Streisand effect is a social phenomenon that occurs when an attempt to hide, remove, or censor information has the unintended consequence of further publicizing that information.) Nonetheless, use the tools that are adequately provided from the enterprise. Consultation with the legal team can help prevent a minor mishap from escalating into something that is much more serious. Initiating conversations with the legal team should always be used as an absolute last resort. Even if the vulnerability did leak on social media, a program manager must be willing to accept that these types of events happen. Program managers should not default to a thought process of assuming that the hacker is malicious,, but always try to diffuse and understand the hacker. Is the hacker leaking the vulnerability on social media purely because they believe they are not getting a fair or swift response? Is the program's communication good, but the hacker wants an absurd amount of money? Be fair. When a program manager puts themselves in a hacker's shoes, it's easier to have better interactions – even if they seem like a threat actor at first.

It may not always be possible to prevent exploitation, and in a carefully planned scenario in which the researcher was not satisfied with the outcome, it can prove quite deadly. Therefore, it's advisable to maintain good communication and keep adequate documentation of reported vulnerabilities and pertinent information.

5.3 Service Level Agreements (SLAs)

A service level agreement, or SLA, is the enterprise's promise to a researcher to respond to or to fix the reported vulnerability in an adequate amount of time. Private bug bounty programs can benefit from providing both report triage times and vulnerability patching times. When a program grows, times may need to be shifted, or in specific scenarios pulled out altogether. One solid affirmation that can be made about the triage or resolution process: no matter whether times are defined or not, it's 100% safe to assume that at some given point a researcher is going to ask either when their vulnerability is going to be looked at or when a triaged vulnerability will be fixed.

How does one accurately build a model for resolution or triage times? Most of the crowdsourcing platforms will have recommended best practices outlined for adequate triage process, especially if the platform is going to be providing managed services. However, in the event that the enterprise does not choose to go with a managed service model or avoids using a crowdsourced solution altogether, all of the possible scenarios should be known.

It's difficult to determine what model will be best for a given enterprise. Consider the following:

- Is the program private or public? If it's public, set realistic expectations. Can every medium vulnerability be resolved by the enterprise in seven days or less?
- How well do the software engineers know how to patch bugs? It's no surprise that bugs are going to have to be fixed by these engineers. If they don't understand secure coding models, it's impossible to provide adequate resolution timeframes.
- Have statistics for the program been analyzed? As stated earlier in the book, launching a public program from the jump typically isn't an effective way to evaluate the necessary adjustments and build a decent program. Although it's not impossible, it's

not recommended. If a program manager starts with a private program, it's easier to get accustomed to the workflow and determine SLA estimates. Security has never been a race – it's a marathon.

Although there are several ways to line up SLA agreements, here are some examples to assist in the brainstorming process.

5.3.1 Resolution Times

Misconceptions exist about bug bounty program resolution times. A lot of security researchers believe that missing a resolution time represents a disastrous program, and it's up to program managers to fix these misconceptions. Defining adequate time ranges that the program knows engineering teams can hold themselves accountable to in regards to vulnerability resolution is an important part of program management. By creating such resolution ranges, program managers have more flexibility to be transparent with researchers.

As an additional note, most bug bounty platforms auto-populate average resolution times, issues resolved, and so on. Most researchers can deduce the level of effort and responsibility exercised by the program from these statistics. However, providing a table helps a researcher compare averages against SLA and, if done properly, it can inspire more participation in a program (see Table 5.1).

Defining an SLA directly in a program is best done when the enterprise can properly establish it without guesswork. The possibility of a bug falling out of the team's purview could happen, and missing an SLA can hurt a program's reputation, but it shouldn't be a discouraging factor for program managers.

5.3.2 Triage Times

Triage times are different in the sense that most bug bounty platforms can manage them on behalf of the researcher if the program decides to go with a managed service model. Nonetheless, if a standalone program is established or an enterprise has to establish its own resolution criteria, an example of possible triage times is displayed in Table 5.2. Triage doesn't typically require a wide range, unless the bug bounty program is exceedingly large.

Table 5.1 Resolution Times for Identified Vulnerabilities.

Vulnerability Rating	Resolution Time
Critical	2–7 days
High	7–14 days
Medium	14–30 days
Low	Best effort
Informational	N/A

Table 5.2 Triage Times for Identified Vulnerabilities.

Vulnerability Rating	Resolution Time
Critical	2 days
High	5 days
Medium	7 days
Low	14 days
Informational	N/A

Validating vulnerabilities doesn't typically take that long. The most difficult portion of the process is the resolution as it requires multitenant collaboration.

The time ranges of all these processes should be adjusted according to program need.

6

Program Configuration

6.1   Understanding Options

The time has finally come to configure a program. This chapter focuses on all of the various options available. Realistically, a step-by-step setup process is less likely to be as useful as a chapter that describes all of the available options. To best configure a program for the enterprise environment, knowing all of the various techniques available will make the bug bounty program far more successful. A lot of engineers setting up programs stray from the options that are within easy reach. Specifically, the objective of this chapter is not to focus on one crowdsourcing platform, but instead to evaluate the options to adequately prepare program managers for a more successful setup. Nonetheless, the various options between Bugcrowd and HackerOne will be presented.

6.2   Bugcrowd

6.2.1   Creating the Program

When first signing up on Bugcrowd's platform, the program manager has the option to choose the program or service they want to use. For our example, we will be choosing between vulnerability disclosure and bug bounty programs. First, the program manager will click on the blue "Start now" button which pulls up the list of the given options.

1. Click on "Start now" (Figure 6.1)

Figure 6.1   Bugcrowd "Start now" button.

Corporate Cybersecurity: Identifying Risks and the Bug Bounty Program, First Edition. John Jackson.
© 2021 John Wiley & Sons, Ltd. Published 2021 by John Wiley & Sons, Ltd.

2. Choose "Bug Bounty Program" by clicking the "Start now" button (Figure 6.2).

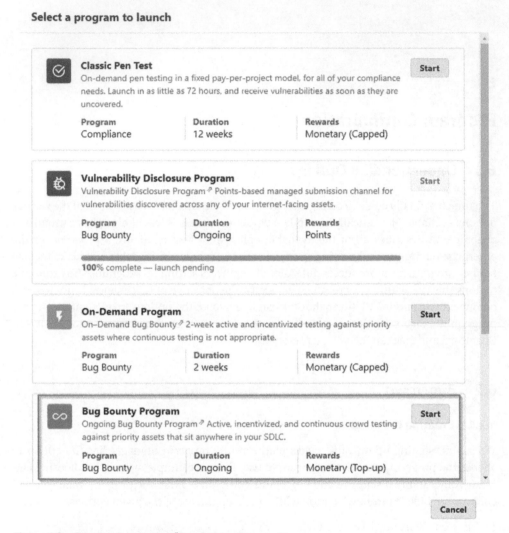

Figure 6.2 Bugcrowd: selection "Bug Bounty Program".

3. Once the start button is clicked, a basic program configuration wizard will populate. The details that are defined can always be changed later, so do not worry too much about getting everything right.

4. When the program wizard comes up, it will show all of the various steps. In total, there are 9. Step 1 focuses on naming the program. The program name should be the name of the company that the program manager will be in charge of (Figure 6.3).

Step 1: Program name

A Bug Bounty is a security testing program that relies on a monetary reward scheme to incentivize members of our white hat hacking community to hunt for high-impact vulnerabilities in a defined set of assets and applications.

The information you provide will help inform program scope and reward range, as well as help us identify the right skills and experience from the crowd to ensure maximum program value.

Launch a Bug Bounty Program

0% complete

→ 1. Program name

2. Set targets

3. Participation guidelines

4. Reward range

5. Identify vulnerability concerns

6. Select your crowd

7. Add look and feel

8. Schedule launch

9. Review and submit

Program Name

This name will identify your program on our platform, as well as inform the URL where it can be accessed directly i.e. www.bugcrowd.com/programs/yourname.

examplecompanyname

Next step

Figure 6.3   Selecting the program name on Bugcrowd.

5. Next, targets, or "assets," will be set for testing. Again, it is OK if only limited assets are added. At this point, it's not necessary to add every asset (Figure 6.4).

Add targets to test

Targets you add will appear here. You can add as many targets as you like and edit them here as necessary.

Add target

Previous step

Next step

Figure 6.4   Adding targets to test on Bugcrowd.

6. Clicking the "Add target" button will bring up the dialog that allows a wide array of asset selections.

7. Now, targets can be added and options can be selected from the dropdown (Figure 6.5). The name represents what you would like to call the asset, keeping in mind that the researcher will see this. Tags can now be selected. Utilizing tagging is essential because it gives the security researcher the best chance of having the correct expertise for conducting research. Next, the URL/location defines where you should expect the researcher to begin testing. Finally, the category helps you define what type of asset it is. Many researchers will look at the category right away and determine if it's the right type of research for them. Be sure to make an adequate effort to label all assets correctly; there's no use in rushing the assets. Click "Add," which will then populate the target on the list. Adding as many as necessary. Click the "Next step" button and proceed.

Figure 6.5 Adding a target to Bugcrowd.

8. Step 3 focuses on the bug bounty program participation guidelines. The first slider allows a program manager to enable or disable Bugcrowd's rating taxonomy. The specific guide outlining all of Bugcrowd's ratings can be seen under the block of text. It's highly recommended that a program manager use this taxonomy rating. Bugcrowd has been managing security research since 2011 and the VRT (vulnerability rating taxonomy) that they use is well maintained, frequently updated as new vulnerabilities are discovered, and reassessed. Alternatively, this can be turned off and self-maintained, but this is not recommended. The next slider allows the program to accept reported issues that are adjacent to nontarget issues, or in other words imagine a researcher finds an API (application programming interface; a component that defines interactions between multiple software applications or mixed hardware/software intermediaries) key on www.example.com that allows them to interact with login.example.com. If the login subdomain is not in scope, and this slider is disabled, a researcher will not have the opportunity to report the vulnerability. It is recommended to allow researchers to report out of scope, even though it is noted that they will not be rewarded for the vulnerability. The third slider enables or disables safe harbor. Program managers also have the option to select a partial or full safe harbor if the slider is enabled. The entire point of setting up a bug bounty program is giving security researchers a safe haven to hack while improving the effectiveness of the enterprise security posture. Program managers should enable the safe harbor option. Last, the fourth and final slider of this section is the coordinated disclosure option. Enabling this slider gives the researcher the ability to request that their findings be published to the public. This option should be turned on. Security researchers that hack on a program put in their hard work to disclose to get paid and disclose to the public. If a program manager feels as if they are not ready to have patched vulnerabilities disclosed to the world, running a bug bounty program will prove futile. Silence is the exact opposite of what is needed to encourage the growth of an already fragile relationship between hackers and enterprises.

9. In step 4, reward ranges are defined (Figure 6.6). Choose the “Basic” radio button, especially if this is the first time managing a bug bounty program. Additionally, using the maximum advertised reward feature is unnecessary for a program starting out. Tweaking the reward amounts will come with time as vulnerabilities harden the enterprise security posture. Once the radio button is selected, click on the “Next step” button.

Reward ranges by severity
The payment ranges researchers can expect based on technical severity.
Set the program reward range based on the security maturity of your assets.
Basic
Intermediate
Advanced
Technical severity
Low reward
High reward
Critical
Severe
Moderate
Low
Informational
Maximum advertised reward

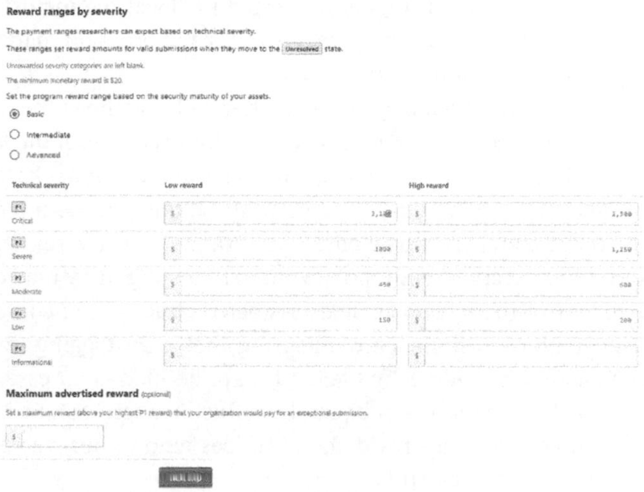

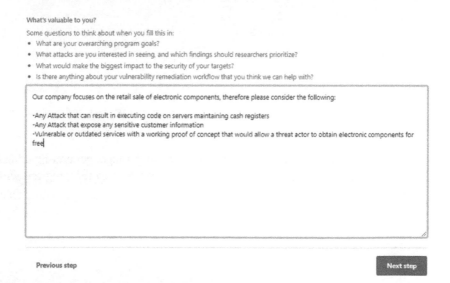

Figure 6.6 Adding reward ranges by severity on Bugcrowd.

10. In step 5, program managers should describe what ideal research concerns look like. Describing areas of focus will help security researchers get a better understanding of what the enterprise is trying to accomplish, for example imagine if a retail company runs a bounty program. They may write something like this (Figure 6.7):

What's valuable to you?
Some questions to think about when you fill this in:
• What are your overarching program goals?
• What attacks are you interested in seeing, and which findings should researchers prioritize?
• What would make the biggest impact to the security of your targets?
• Is there anything about your vulnerability remediation workflow that you think we can help with?
Our company focuses on the retail sale of electronic components, therefore please consider the following:
-Any Attack that can result in executing code on servers maintaining cash registers
-Any Attack that expose any sensitive customer information
-Vulnerable or outdated services with a working proof of concept that would allow a threat actor to obtain electronic components for free
Previous step
Next step

Figure 6.7 Identify goals and concerns on Bugcrowd.

As a small example, some considerations focus on cash registers, exposure of sensitive customer data, and any vulnerabilities that can result in the theft of sensitive information. It's highly important to tell researchers what the program is looking for. However, note that researchers will still attempt to research whatever they want if not explicitly stated as out of scope (and sometimes even still, if it is). Additionally, feel free to focus on specific classes of attacks instead of vectors of attack such as telling researchers that the program is highly interested in "local file inclusion" or "remote code execution," and so on. This is a great space for the program manager to describe all of the important versus unimportant aspects.

11. Step 6 is the technical tagging follow-through after defining the vulnerabilities that the bug bounty program is concerned with. There are four sections of the tagging process: researcher activities, asset environments, languages and frameworks, and hosted and third-party applications (Figure 6.8). Defining these tags can be important as it can help the correct researchers participate. For example, if a researcher sees that a program is mostly concerned with mobile and API testing, they may decide that it is not for them, saving them a great deal of wasted time and encouraging the right research demographics to participate. Ensuring that asset tagging, research desires, and various frameworks and desired activities are defined is an essential process to help ensure that the program is adequately defined. Programs are free to limit the amount of information that is provided, but it does tend to hurt the general security stance and waste a researcher's time.

Figure 6.8 Select researcher activities, environments, languages, frameworks, and applications/services.

12. Next is "Adding the look and feel" – in short, uploading a logo, generating a tagline that will go under the program, and welcoming researchers to the program with a short description (Figure 6.9).

Figure 6.9 Upload your company's logo and create a tagline and introduction.

Additionally, a background color can be chosen for the logo, so give it the best attempt at a decent contrast to make it pop to a security researcher. The introduction space is nothing more than explaining who the program is and why they are hiring security researchers. The space can also be used to explain what the company does and their mission. Inspiring researchers to participate is the ultimate goal.

13. Step 8 focuses on defining a timeline for both a private and a public launch. If the program manager has already reached the phase of setting up the program, it typically indicates a certain level of readiness and a commitment to setting up a program. For the "Preferred private launch timeline" it is recommended to prepare to launch "Within a month." As program managers tend to learn, a public program launch is a far bigger commitment. Program managers should select the "More than a month after private launch" option as there will be plenty of work to accomplish to enable a public launch.

14. Finally, when the next button is clicked in step 8, a page will populate that highlights all of the incentives. Review all of the submitted information and click "Submit" when ready to move on to the next phase.

6.2.2 Program Overview

Now that the program is fully set up, getting a feel for the various options and functionality is the next step in understanding how to manage a bug bounty program. Program managers should get familiar with all of the various pages and each of the ways to modify existing program settings to prevent any issues when the program goes live.

6.2.2.1 The Program Dashboard

Once the bug bounty program is created, it brings the program manager back to the dashboard in which they started. The dashboard allows the creation of additional programs but also allows program managers to click on a "Tasks" or the "Welcome center" tab (Figure 6.10). The tasks tab allows program managers to see a quick overview of all the to-do vulnerabilities within all of the programs, or even filter by specific programs.

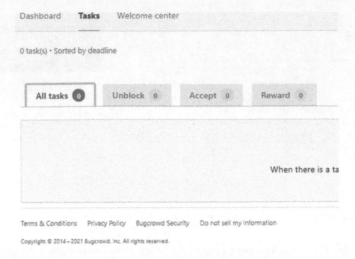

Figure 6.10 Vulnerability tasking tabs.

As seen, the program manager can see if there are any blockers or vulnerabilities that need to be dealt with or rewarded.

The welcome center promotes all the various Bugcrowd documentation (Figure 6.11), including various videos to help program managers effectively run a bug bounty program. The welcome center can assist in leading a program in the right direction. If ever a program manager needs ideas to upgrade the program, fix common configuration issues, or understand the breadth of the vulnerability research space, the welcome center is the hub for knowledge. The welcome center contains hours of videos, manuals, questions, and studies highlighting best practices for managing effective programs. Program managers can benefit from taking the time to read through some of the documentation and to watch the included

Figure 6.11 Bugcrowd documentation.

videos. While not necessary at first, it wouldn't hurt to get a better understanding of the way Bugcrowd operates.

Figure 6.12   Program dropdown menu.

Returning back to the main screen, there is a program dashboard the program manager can click on the dropdown menu to select the bug bounty program that they would like to manage (Figure 6.12).

6.2.2.2   The Crowd Control Navbar

When a program manager clicks on their program in the dropdown menu, they will be directed to an interface that allows them to manage vulnerabilities and the more advanced configuration settings for the program.

Figure 6.13   Crowd control navbar.

The top panel allows program managers to see a summary of the program, submissions, view and manage researchers, gain insights into the program, and view reports/modify settings (Figure 6.13).

Summary

The summary page shows program managers all of the program's recent activities as well as a quick snapshot of their assigned submissions and status of each submission that is currently within the program. Program managers can use this dashboard as a quick way to navigate to issues that need their attention and to get a general feel for the remediation processes and steps needed to push their program into an adequate state.

Submissions

The submissions panel is a more extensive version of the summary page (Figure 6.14). This page can be used for more advanced filtering of issues and allows program managers to

Figure 6.14 Vulnerability submissions panel.

have a much wider view of all of the submitted vulnerabilities and resolve them effectively. Program managers also have the option to download all of the submissions as a CSV file for tracking and sorting.

Researchers

The researchers web page shows a total of all the researchers that have been invited, have submitted to the program, the total submissions, and the valid submissions. Underneath the totals, a program manager can see the participating researchers (Figure 6.15).

Figure 6.15 Program participants tab.

Additionally, the "Invitations" tab allows program managers to invite researchers by email. Details of the researcher will not be revealed, to maintain a good privacy posture and allow the researcher to stay safe (Figure 6.16).

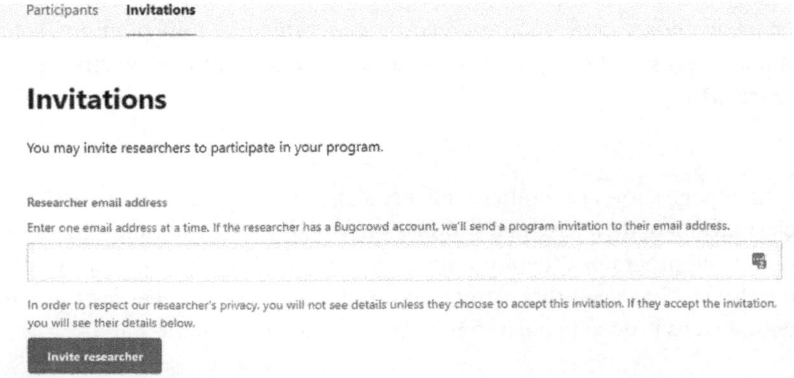

Participants **Invitations**

Invitations

You may invite researchers to participate in your program.

Researcher email address

Enter one email address at a time. If the researcher has a Bugcrowd account, we'll send a program invitation to their email address.

In order to respect our researcher's privacy, you will not see details unless they choose to accept this invitation. If they accept the invitation, you will see their details below.

Invite researcher

Figure 6.16 Program invitations tab.

Rewards

The rewards tab allows program managers to see the various metrics as they pertain to researcher rewards. A quick summary shows how many rewards were given out, the highest reward achieved, the average monetary amount given out, and the remaining reward pool. Program managers have the option to change the length of time that is evaluated in the upper-right-hand corner, and the "Reward History" will provide all of the researchers that were awarded in a given period (Figure 6.17). Program managers also have the option to download this as a CSV file. The rewards tab is useful as it allows higher-level management to analyze trends and project expansion and reward predictions.

Figure 6.17   Program rewards dashboard.

Insights Dashboard

The insights dashboard provides an overview of various trends and allows program managers to view valuable data and charts that help them understand the bug bounty program better (Figure 6.18). For example, the severity trend of reports and the volume of reports received can be viewed. Additionally, there are performance metrics, amounts paid to researchers by target, and an overall target breakdown (Figures 6.19 and 6.20).

Figure 6.18   Insights dashboard: technical severity chart.

Figure 6.19   Insights dashboard: target breakdown.

Performance
Average times to transition vulnerabilities.

Days in triage	Days in review	Days to fix
8.6	14.6	38.4

Transition times by severity

Technical Severity	Days to Triage	Days in Review	Days To Fix
Critical	0.0 days	--	90.0 days
Severe	0.0 days	29.1 days	0.0 days
Moderate	5.9 days	--	65.0 days
Low	18.6 days	0.0 days	--
Informational	--	--	--
None	--	--	--

Figure 6.20   Insights dashboard: performance.

Reports

In the reports tab, program managers can generate reports on their program summary, program health and spend, and security posture reports. Program managers should occasionally generate and review these reports as it will assist in establishing a great deal of information on every aspect of their program.

Review the Bugcrowd link for a more granular overview on reporting and instructions for doing so: https://docs.bugcrowd.com/customers/program-management/generating-reports/#program-summary-report.

6.2.3   Advanced Program Configuration and Modification

All of the program settings from the initial setup can be modified. While the "Settings" tab is part of the crowd control navbar, there are many aspects to cover that warrant this tab having its own section in this chapter.

6.2.3.1   Program Brief

The program brief web page is the first visual that a program manager will see when clicking on the "Settings" tab. Essentially, the program brief contains the basic settings of the bug bounty program (Figure 6.21). These settings were established when the program was

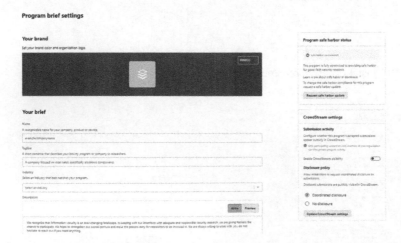

Figure 6.21   Program brief settings.

first made, such as the program's name, tagline, disclosure policy, safe harbor, etc. If any updates to the general program need to be made, this is the section that will be utilized.

6.2.3.2 Scope and Rewards

The scope and rewards section is a more visual representation of the program scope details. In this section, the program manager has the specific ability to drill down into more of the details of the focus areas, what assets are out of scope, and modify the safe harbor as they see fit. Additionally, the ability to discuss the specifics of rewards for in- and out-of-scope assets can be discussed here. The scope and rewards sections may seem redundant, but the purpose is to express the enterprise's stance to ensure that the researcher is aware of all of the possibilities. For example, earlier during the initial configuration the scope and rewards were set. However, this would be a good section to use as a venue to explain to the researcher specifics of the scope as the enterprise may have specific ideas in mind. Take a look at the following screenshot (Figure 6.22):

Figure 6.22 Scope details.

As seen in Figure 6.22 under the target information section, a defined credential pair has been provided for testing purposes. In addition, the same figure highlights areas that the enterprise is also concerned with, as an example. Finally, this section is closed out with a custom "Out-of-Scope" notes section. The scope details section is not to be taken lightly, because a failure to handle this section carefully can result in mishaps such as a researcher attempting an attack that can be detrimental to employee safety or the enterprise environment. A program manager should strive to carefully review the ideal out-of-scope attacks in Chapter 4 and also review the various out-of-scope sections of some of the other public bug bounty programs that are out there to get a good idea of what the enterprise should strive to avoid. For the most part, triage will assist in explaining to a researcher the issues that surround low-level vulnerabilities or those that lack impact. However, the problem lies with valid vulnerabilities that the enterprise bug bounty program may not want to accept. Imagine the following.

The program manager knows that the enterprise is riddled with cross-site scripting (XSS) vulnerabilities. All of the software engineers are aware that nearly every parameter on the domain has issues with XSS. The enterprise still wants to utilize a private bug bounty program but areas of focus are on vulnerabilities that are not well known as issues, such as local file inclusion, remote code execution, html injection, etc. If the program manager did not consider the cleverness of the hackers that will be invited to the program, they may end up with a massive amount of XSS reports – and because it wasn't marked as an out-of-scope vulnerability type, it could result in the bug bounty program having to pay a lot of money to researchers. One of the most important aspects of program management is realizing that saying, "Ah, we should have had this in our out-of-scope section," is not an acceptable response by any means and the enterprise will be on the hook for it.

For the most part, the premade safe harbor section is decent and should be kept. Nonetheless, program managers should talk to management to ensure that everyone is on the same page and that the safe harbor adequately reflects the needs of the enterprise. Still, program managers should not let upper-level management or legal teams fully control the safe harbor clause or additions to such clauses, as the result may be overbearing and dissuasive to security researchers who may want to participate.

A "Target Groups" section also exists in this section. It can be a useful way to organize similar assets to prevent researchers from smashing their keyboard attempting to look at all of the tags for what they are hoping to test. Logically, a program manager will want to add all relevant assets before making the group. Unfortunately, to do so, a different section of the application must be utilized. Follow these instructions:

1. Click on the profile image in the top-right-hand corner and then click on the "Targets" tab under the bug bounty program name (Figure 6.23):

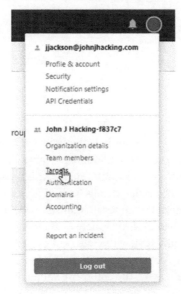

Figure 6.23 Profile dropdown menu.

2. Clicking on the "Targets" option brings up a web page that acts similar to the initial targets page as discussed when the program was initially set up (Figure 6.24). This would be a good time to add and tag any additional assets that researchers should test.

Note: remember that not every asset needs to be added at once. If the program manager only has a couple of targets at first, or does not have a lot of assets that can be similarly grouped – that's fine! As the program expands, groups can be utilized. In fact, there's no harm in establishing the groups as is with minimal assets just to keep everything organized for the future.

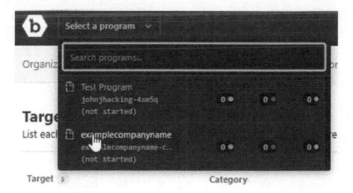

Figure 6.24 Targets tab.

3. After adding all of the relevant assets, as seen above, return to the scope and rewards section by clicking on the "Select a program" dropdown menu and selecting the program (Figure 6.25).

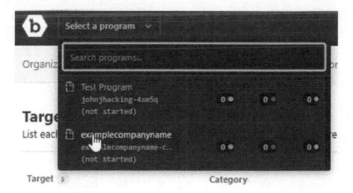

Figure 6.25 Program dropdown menu.

4. Again, click on the "Settings" tab on the crowd control navbar, as done previously. Then click on the "Scope and Rewards" tab and, lastly, the "Target Groups" tab.

Adding the groups can be simple but daunting and turn into a mess if the program manager isn't ready to do so. In reality, the option of group utilization is useful for adjusting reward levels, and can be used to turn out-of-scope reporting into in-scope reporting with benefits. To add a group, perform the following.

1. First, click on the "Add group" button (Figure 6.26).

ᵗ. Use 'Out of scope' groups to

Figure 6.26 "Add group" button.

2. A target group web page will populate. For the title, it is recommended to use something broad to prevent an overwhelming amount of groups from being created. As an example, having general categories such as "Web Application Testing," "Network Testing," "Mobile Application Testing," "API Testing," etc., will give security researchers a better sense of what to test. However, it isn't a necessity, and program managers can use more granular names depending on the specific case. After the title is added, a description of the asset group can be useful for security researchers (Figure 6.27).

Figure 6.27 Description of an asset group.

3. The next portion underneath the description box is a checkbox that asks if the target group is in scope (Figure 6.28). Clicking on the checkbox reveals another checkbox that asks the program manager if the asset group "pays monetary rewards." The checkbox for rewards is a useful component of target groups, because program managers can take assets that would normally be considered out of scope and offer a limited in-scope option. For example, if the enterprise maintains a domain that is highly vulnerable, leaving the "pays monetary rewards" option unchecked but adding the assets can allow researchers to test and report the vulnerabilities, and the enterprise will not have to pay for the asset. The official recommendation would be to eventually put the assets in scope when they are considered less vulnerable.

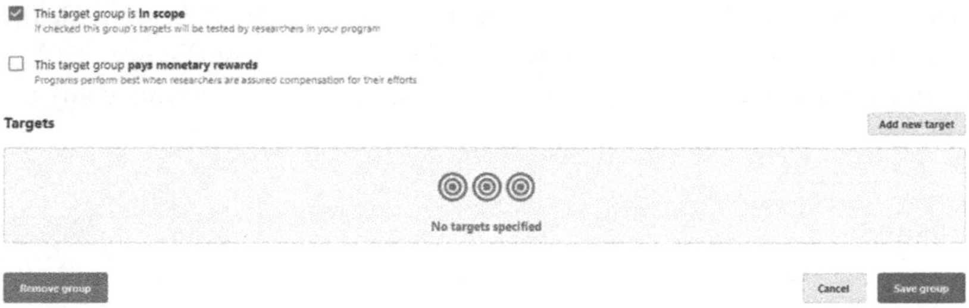

Figure 6.28 Target groups.

For this current example, the "Network Assets" group is being created. Therefore, the example that is going to be shown is the result of enabling monetary rewards to walk through the process of creating and modifying rewards.

4. With the checkbox clicked for the rewards option, an overlay will pop up, showing various reward options for the group, such as tiers ranked at high, medium, low, and custom (Figure 6.29). These brackets have price ranges on each, and the custom tier can be used for defining rewards per vulnerability criticality classification. Groups are unique in the sense that multiple groups can be assigned different tiers, therefore making it worth a researcher's time to hack mobile applications over web applications, etc.

Figure 6.29 Target group rewards.

5. After the reward is selected, a program manager must click on the "Add new target" button. The only option that is different with this interface is the ability to pick pre-existing targets and add them to the group. Adding each target to a specific group will have to be completely individually. Once all of the targets are added, a program manager can click on the "Save group" button, which will bring program managers to the next web page.

6. Finally, the groups will be populated on the "Target groups" page, with the name, rewards, and all of the details that were assigned previously (Figure 6.30). Program managers will have to utilize the "Add group" option in order to make any additional groups.

Figure 6.30 Target group listings.

6.2.3.3 Integrations

The integrations tab of the settings option allows program managers to connect any relevant tools that their enterprise might have for managing reports (Figure 6.31). For example, various configurations such as Jira, Slack, ServiceNow, etc., exist – allowing for an effective reporting and triage workflow. Program managers can opt to use none of these tools, or many of these tools. A standard integration flow may be a ticketing system tool such as Jira, Slack notifications to bring a program manager's attention to the submission, or an

Figure 6.31 Integrating various tools to help with report management.

embedded submission form on the website that gives the enterprise the ability to receive submissions from anyone if they don't exclusively know about Bugcrowd's services.

Rather than explain each integration, program managers are encouraged to review the Bugcrowd documentation. The integration process will vary based on the type of tool Bugcrowd is integrating with.

6.2.3.4 Announcements

The "Announcements" tab is used for notifying researchers of major changes within the program (Figure 6.32). Examples of an adequate usage of announcements would be: Increasing Rewards, Expanding Scope, Asking researchers to test a specific asset, etc.

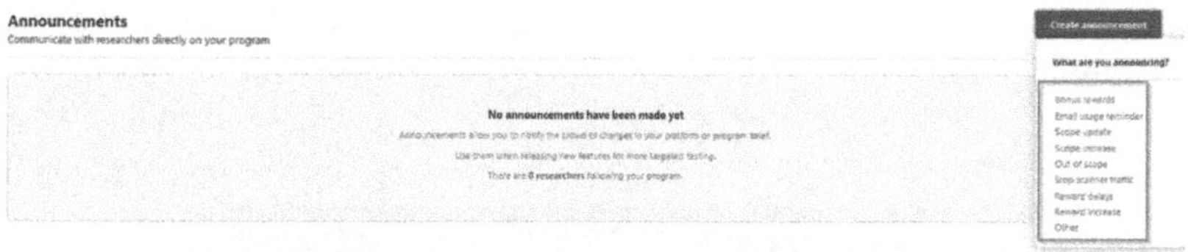

Figure 6.32 Announcements option.

In addition, Bugcrowd maintains specific premade templates that can be used as a starting point for notifying researchers such as Email usage reminders, Scope updates, Reward delays, and more. As you can see in Figure 6.33, the premade templates can be written and the publish announcement button can be pressed to announce the program's message to all researchers.

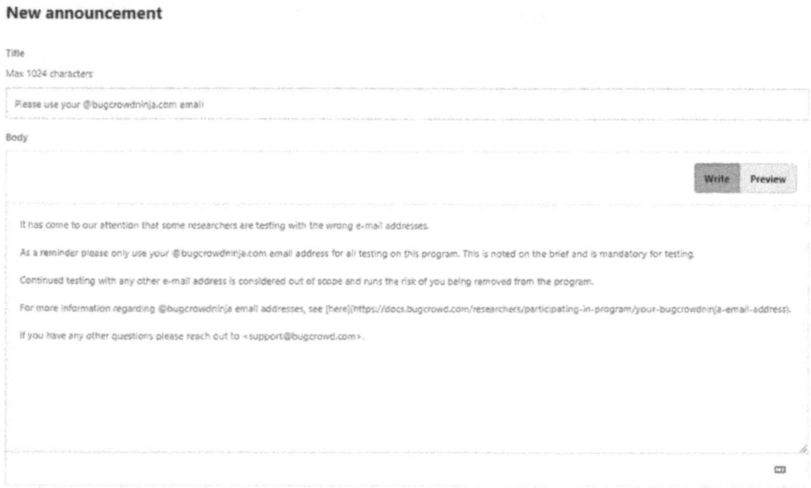

Figure 6.33 New announcement option.

6.2.3.5 Manage Team

In the manage team section, program managers can invite team members to assist in managing the program (Figure 6.34). Additionally, the settings allow for an auto assignment of triaged or critical tickets which can assist employees in responding to issues faster, especially if it's necessary to do so quickly.

Manage team

planetxort
jjackson@jshrjhacking.com

Owner | ⌄   Remove

Figure 6.34 Manage team option.

Beyond seeing the existing team members, program managers can invite team members by clicking on the "Invite a team member" button, and additionally assign the roles as discussed. (Figure 6.35).

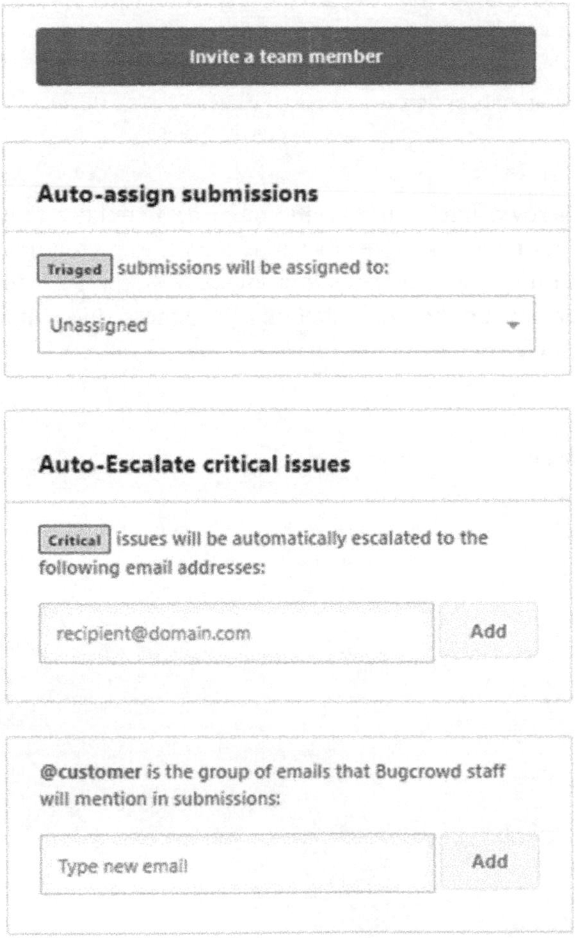

> **Invite a team member**
>
> **Auto-assign submissions**
>
> Triaged submissions will be assigned to:
>
> Unassigned ▼
>
> **Auto-Escalate critical issues**
>
> Critical issues will be automatically escalated to the following email addresses:
>
> recipient@domain.com   Add
>
> @customer is the group of emails that Bugcrowd staff will mention in submissions:
>
> Type new email   Add

Figure 6.35 Invite a team member option.

Three separate roles exist when the invite button is pressed: Admin, Analyst, and Viewer. The Admin role can do anything within the program. The Analyst can only manage submissions and basic settings, and the Viewer can only review submissions and options within the program.

6.2.3.6 Submissions

The final program settings tab is the "Submissions" tab. One of the options that can be utilized is a data fields option. This allows program managers to create custom submission fields that can only be seen internally. The fields can be useful in the instance where vulnerabilities need to be easily identified and tagged with a message that the entire team has the ability to see. For example, data fields such as "No Impact" or "Special Exception" could be useful to internally relay that a ticket may be a false-positive or a vulnerability that was brought from out of scope to in scope (Figure 6.36). The options are limitless and program managers should experiment and brainstorm with team members to come up with useful data field options.

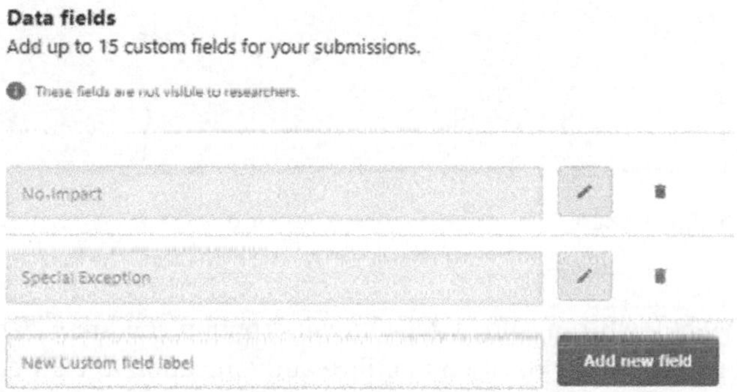

Figure 6.36 Data fields option.

Next, the CVSS v3 score option is the same as the initial configuration of the program (Figure 6.37). Enabling this option allows for Bugcrowd's scoring and metric system for the various vulnerabilities.

Figure 6.37 CVSS v3 option.

The remediation advice option should be enabled. There's no logical reason not to have it enabled as the researcher cannot see the advice and it is a useful feature (Figure 6.38). If the option becomes redundant, it can be turned off in the same way that it was turned on.

Remediation advice
Include advice on how to remediate vulnerabilities on each submission.

🛈 These fields are not visible to researchers.

Enable remediation advice

Figure 6.38 Remediation advice option.

After the remediation advice option is the ability to enable retesting. To be honest, the option is up to the discretion of the program manager. When engineers gain more experience, it's unlikely that they will need assistance with retesting. Nonetheless, it could be a useful option for new program managers. However, it should not be relied upon. One of the best ways to learn the ins and outs of a program is to be on top of testing the vulnerabilities submitted by the researcher. If the program manager constantly tests the vulnerabilities, it's unlikely that they will need to pay researchers for retesting (Figure 6.39).

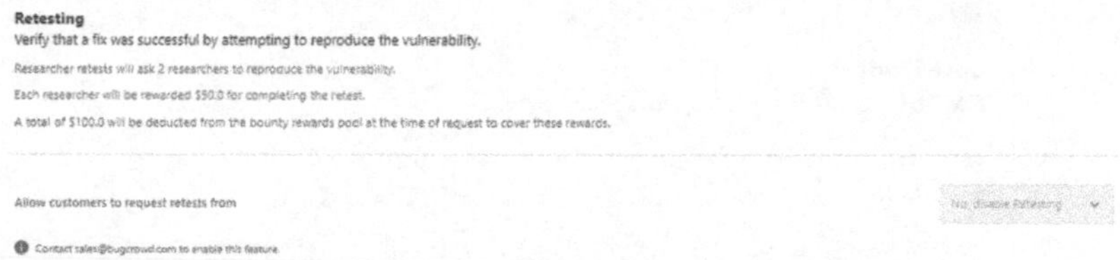

Retesting
Verify that a fix was successful by attempting to reproduce the vulnerability.

Researcher retests will ask 2 researchers to reproduce the vulnerability.

Each researcher will be rewarded $50.0 for completing the retest.

A total of $100.0 will be deducted from the bounty rewards pool at the time of request to cover these rewards.

Allow customers to request retests from

🛈 Contact sales@bugcrowd.com to enable this feature.

Figure 6.39 Retesting option.

Last is the "Markdown Embedded Attachments" option (Figure 6.40). If this option is enabled, it will require the application to utilize authentication to view embedded images. Leaving this on is important if a program manager values the security of their enterprise.

Markdown Embedded Attachments
Allows users to attach and embed images directly into submission Markdown fields and comments.

This setting can be used when you need embedded attachments to be viewable from an external integration.

Figure 6.40 Markdown embedded attachments option.

6.2.4 Profile Settings

The final part of the Bugcrowd platform (loosely stated, as there's much to learn) is the "Profile and Enterprise" sidebar which also includes some payment and good housekeeping functionality (Figure 6.41). Among the settings is the ability to refine account security, utilize API credentials, and manage the program's accounting capabilities. Program managers should immediately tune their profile settings to adequately secure their program login. Maintaining best security practice for the bug bounty program login itself is arguably just as important as resolving the vulnerabilities. If a threat actor were to get access to the bug bounty program login, they would be able to see all of the pre-existing bugs. Therefore, securing any associated accounts registered to the program is not to be taken lightly.

Figure 6.41 Profile and enterprise sidebar.

The first aspect, "Profile", includes the settings that are under the email address of the user that is logged into the program. Here, the program manager has the ability to modify profile and account settings, security settings, notification settings, and generate API credentials that can interact with Bugcrowd's API (Figure 6.42).

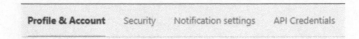

Figure 6.42   Profile option.

6.2.4.1   The Profile and Account

This tab is the default view, and to be frank there's not much that needs to be explained about this tab. Program managers can expect all of the basic functionality such as modifying profile settings, such as name and display name, and changing their passwords or uploading profile pictures.

6.2.4.2   Security

Modifying the profile security settings is the first aspect of profile management that a program manager should do. The "Security" tab allows for a review of individual sessions, or in other words the ability to see where the account is logged in (Figure 6.43).

Figure 6.43   Security option.

The next tab is "Events," which can be used as a method of additional telemetry into sessions which could allude to suspicious activity (Figure 6.44).

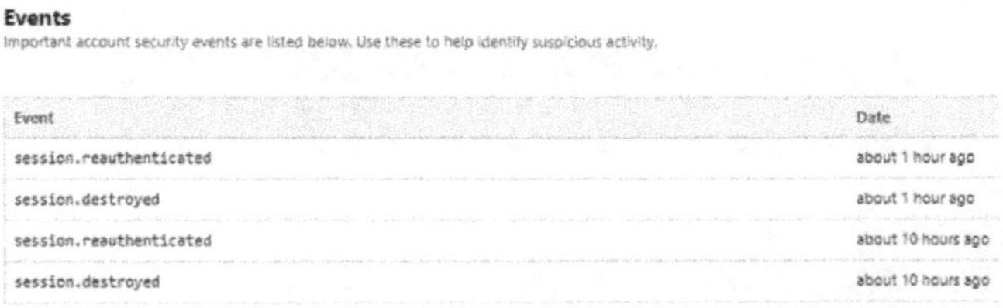

Figure 6.44   Events option.

Last, but not least, two-factor authentication is the actual security configuration setting that can be utilized (Figure 6.45). Setting up two-factor authentication is fairly simple. A program manager will install a two-factor authentication app, such as Google Authenticator, on their mobile device and scan the corresponding QR code or manually enter the code into the app. The final part to enable is to type in a generated six-digit OTP code and click on the "Enable 2FA button." While using two-factor authentication can seem pesky, it's important to do so to protect enterprise bug reports, which, if exposed, could lead to compromised assets.

Figure 6.45 Two-factor authentication option.

6.2.4.3 Notification Settings

A program manager has full transparency and control over the notifications that they will receive from the bug bounty program. Tuning the notifications panel should be an important priority to program managers. Otherwise, "alert fatigue" may occur, or in other words an overwhelming feeling of having too much to look at (Figure 6.46). Preventing alert fatigue through managing notifications is an aspect of engineering that is frequently overlooked. Imagine a home alarm system that also has cameras and alerts based on a ruleset. If the homeowner gets an alert twenty times a day, it may feel burdensome and could result in their ignoring an actual event that needs to be reviewed. The same considerations go for alert management.

As can be seen in Figure 6.46, there's quite a bit to unpack, but it's actually less than one would imagine. For example, the email notification options are straightforward, allowing a program manager to receive emails during activity on subscribed submissions, when team members @mention them, or when a submission is assigned to their program management account username. Leaving the "Activity on subscribed submissions" turned off is up to the preference of the program manager. If the company isn't exceedingly large, or an engineer's near-full-time role is to manage a bug bounty program, having all of the notifications turned on is likely the best possible decision. As an in-between consideration, "Activity on subscribed submissions" can be set to "on" in conjunction with the "Subscribe me when a submission reaches a given state" to "Triaged." Enabling the in-between consideration as

Notification settings

Email notifications

Choose when you receive email notifications.

Activity on subscribed submissions

Team members @mention me.

Submission is assigned to me.

Subscription settings

Choose when you are subscribed to a submission.

Subscribe me to submissions that I edit or comment on. Also subscribe me if I am @mentioned or assigned to a submission.

Subscribe me when a submission reaches a given state.   Select a state

General activity

Select how you receive notifications of activities.

	None	Web only	Web and email
Someone writes a private comment or researcher replies.	○ None	⦿ Web only	○ Web and email
Submission changes state.	○ None	⦿ Web only	○ Web and email
Researcher is rewarded.	○ None	⦿ Web only	○ Web and email
Researcher requests disclosure.	○ None	○ Web only	⦿ Web and email

Figure 6.46 Notifications settings option.

described will allow program managers to be alerted in the instance of receiving important updates on a ticket that is triaged. However, please note that at times there may be overbearing security researchers, so experimenting with the notifications and tuning until it's right will be a program manager's best bet. Not every program manager has the same preferences. Advice for notifications should be taken in one's stride.

6.2.4.4 API Credentials

Program managers may want to develop workflows that utilize API calls through scripting, or various external tooling. Bugcrowd allows this type of flexibility to occur as engineers, both security and software alike, may want to utilize this feature. Generating an API key is simple. To generate a key, the program manager just has to type the name of the application in the "Application name" field and click on the "Create credentials" button. The credentials will then be generated and will not be accessible after navigating away from the page (Figure 6.47).

API credentials

Using these credentials your organization can create applications that work with our API. Learn more about our API in our developer documentation

Add credentials

Provide an application name. After your credentials are created you can pin your token to an API version below.

Application name

My application   Create credentials

Successfully created credentials for: Custom Resolution Script
Be sure to copy the following credentials. They will not be accessible after navigating away from this page.
HTTP Basic Authentication Username

HTTP Basic Authentication Password

HTTP Authorization Header
Authorization: token

Current credentials

Application name	Default version	Created	Actions
Custom Resolution Script	Level (2021-10-31)	In a few seconds	🗑

Figure 6.47 API credentials option.

6.2.5 Enterprise "Profile" Settings

6.2.5.1 Management and Configuration

The final aspect of Bugcrowd is the ability to reconfigure, set up program authentication, or fund the program with accounting settings. Program managers will have to review and action several of these items, as a bug bounty program offers rewards and a pool of money to pull rewards from, which will need to be allocated.

6.2.5.2 Organization Details

The organization details web page hardly differs from the initial setup. This page allows a program manager to upload a new logo for the organization, changing the background color or adding a contact number for the program.

6.2.5.3 Team Members

The team members page exists on other parts of the program configuration. Therefore, the only thing program managers need to know is that this is another route.

6.2.5.4 Targets

Program managers setting up their first program have already utilized this page, as adding targets was a prerequisite to creating groups for the bug bounty program.

6.2.5.5 Authentication

Aspects of authentication are harder to advise on initially, as it will depend on the way the enterprise structures their IdP (identity provider) management. However, program managers should strive to utilize SSO (single sign-on) where available as it is far safer for the enterprise as a whole. Nearly all of the modern-day SSO solutions require users to have (two-factor authentication)TFA enabled to log in, therefore making a program manager's experience far safer. As an example, Okta is an application that enables the usage of SSO for various applications. Program managers should reach out to their IT support team to find out which team within the organization manages identity management provisioning. There are two aspects of the SSO integration: specific site configuration and SAML (Security Assertion Markup Language) settings. The SSO configuration needs to be provided to the appropriate team to fill in the required fields for the enablement of the solution. In addition, the same team will have to provide the program manager with all of the SAML settings for the identity management provider to fill in the corresponding fields. Once complete, the authentication settings can be saved.

As seen in Figure 6.48, the various fields need to be completed. If the enterprise does not maintain an SSO solution, the Bugcrowd default will be the utilization of a standard enterprise email address in conjunction with a password.

Note: domain verification is needed in order to establish SSO within the program, so the following "Domains" tab setup should be carefully followed.

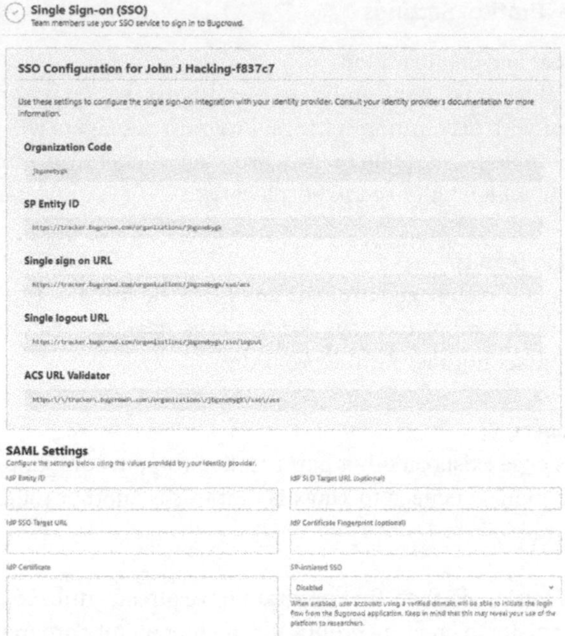

Figure 6.48 Single sign-on option.

6.2.5.6 Domains

Verifying any of the domains added to the program is required to enable SSO. To complete the verification process, all of the domains can be entered in the textbox and the "Add domain" button can be pressed. Once the domain is added, it will populate under the "Unverified domains" section and a program manager will have to communicate with the enterprise team responsible for managing the DNS (domain name server) for the company. Program managers should let the responsible team (which may be the network engineering team or similar) know that they need to verify all of the domains in order to set up SSO. The unverified domains will have a verification code next to them, and the code needs to be added to a TXT (text record, which is a resource record in the domain name system [DNS] used to provide the ability to associate arbitrary text with a host or other name) record and hosted on the root domain (Figure 6.49). It may take 24 hours for it to populate.

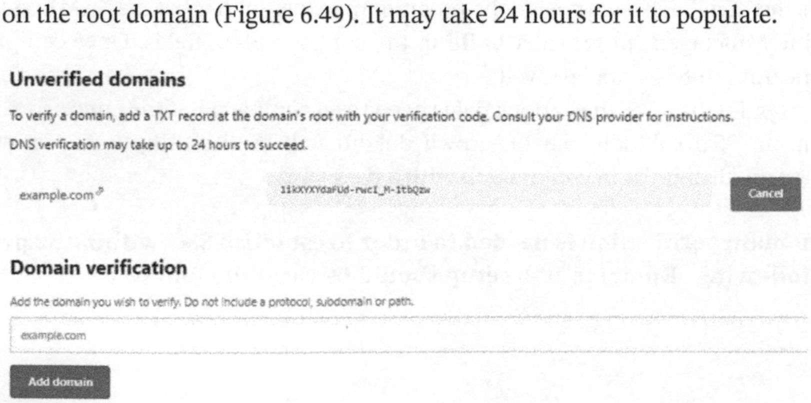

Figure 6.49 Unverified domains option.

6.2.5.7 Accounting

Program managers will utilize the accounting page as a means of allocating a bug bounty pool. Bug bounty program managers can transfer funds, deposit funds, or see an overall activity or program balance. Without a bounty pool assigned, researchers cannot get awarded. Program managers should ensure that this feature is set up before continuing.

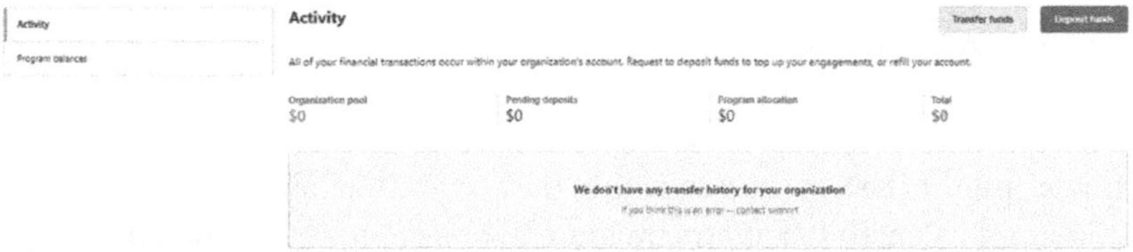

Figure 6.50 Activity summary.

As shown in Figure 6.50, an activity summary is provided, including an organizational pool, pending deposits, program allocation, and total amount of money spent. Program managers can click on the "Deposit funds" button to assign money to their bounty pool.

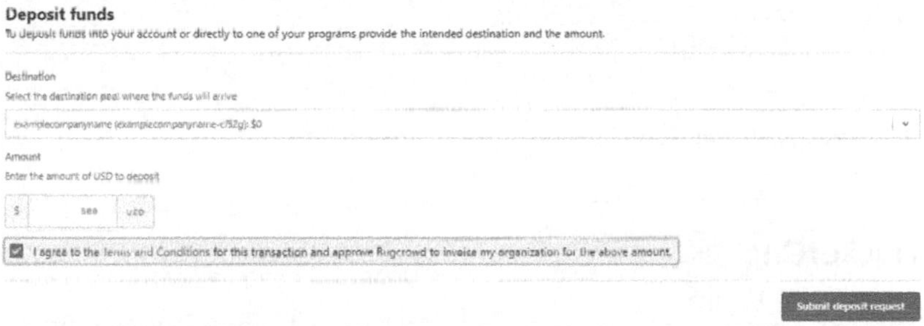

Figure 6.51 Submit deposit request option.

When the "Deposit funds" button is clicked, there will be a textbox that asks for the destination, and that is where the program manager will select the program they would want to assign money to. The program manager can then type the amount of money into the textbox, click on the "I agree to terms and conditions for the transaction" checkbox, and click on the submit deposit request (Figure 6.51). The account manager will then send an invoice to the program manager to run through to the finance team. Program managers will have to ensure that management is tracking expenditures and get it approved through the correct processes. Once Bugcrowd approves the pending deposits, the bug bounty pool will be assigned money that can be used to reward researchers.

Note: program managers should never assume that they have enough money in the pool. It is an essential responsibility to ensure that the program manager is keeping track of the reward pool at all times.

As shown in Figure 6.52, a program manager can also utilize the "Transfer funds" button. Transferring funds allows program managers to deposit money from one pool to another when they run multiple programs. The transfer funds option is nearly identical to the

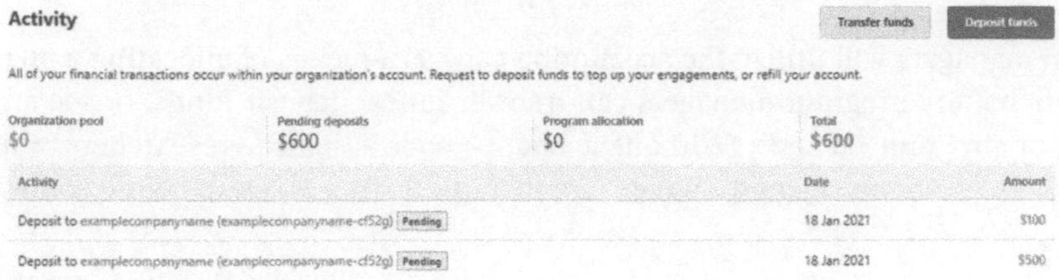

Activity
Transfer funds
Deposit funds
All of your financial transactions occur within your organization's account. Request to deposit funds to top up your engagements, or refill your account.
Organization pool
$0
Pending deposits
$600
Program allocation
$0
Total
$600
Activity
Date
Amount
Deposit to examplecompanyname (examplecompanyname-cf52g) Pending
18 Jan 2021
$100
Deposit to examplecompanyname (examplecompanyname-cf52g) Pending
18 Jan 2021
$500

Figure 6.52 Transfer funds option.

deposit funds option. The final option within the accounting tab is the "Program balances" tab. The program balances tab allows program managers to see the bug bounty pool for a multitude of programs. For example, some enterprises own multiple companies and may want to segment bug bounty programs by company to avoid confusion. When a program manager runs multiple bug bounty programs, they should periodically check the program balances tab to ensure that all of the programs are funded (Figure 6.53).

Activity
Program balances
Program balances
Pool balances for your programs
Name
Balance
examplecompanyname
$0
Test Program
$0

Figure 6.53 Program balances option.

6.3 HackerOne

Another crowdsourcing option is HackerOne. Using HackerOne will feel different from Bugcrowd in the sense that there's more going on, immediately from the login. Specifically, the login to Bugcrowd provides the program manager with a simple overview, whereas HackerOne merges a security researcher's and program manager's views. The merging of research and program views can feel daunting. A new program manager may have issues sorting through the options. Attempting to manage the program can even feel clunky for a more seasoned program manager. However, the intention is to describe most of the functionality available within HackerOne. Additionally, HackerOne has many more options for configuration. However, the expertise of the program manager will determine which crowdsourcing platform is best for them.

Unfortunately, HackerOne does not have an easy-to-utilize demo program that is readily available to anyone. In order to mitigate this issue, an already established program will be utilized and the settings and configurations evaluated. The primary tabs that will be focused on are the program dashboard, program settings, and inbox tabs; anything else within HackerOne typically tends to relate to researchers specifically. Additionally, some of the configuration settings of the profile will be evaluated as well. The ability to understand the setup of a program from start to finish will ultimately result in an easier transition if a program manager ever works for a firm that utilizes a different crowdsourcing platform.

6.3.1 Program Settings

The first aspect that will be focused on is the "Program settings" tab (Figure 6.54). The program settings tab has two subtabs: General and Program. As a baseline, the general tab contains information, product addition, authentication, verified domains, credential management, user management, group management, and an audit log. Additionally, there is a small section dedicated to billing. The program tab has four subheaders with a wide range of options: customization, hacker management, rewards, and automation.

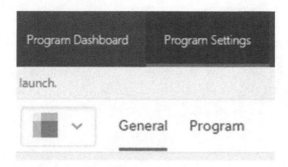

Figure 6.54 Program settings option.

6.3.1.1 General

The general tab can be considered the tab to use when program managers want to configure all of the miscellaneous options of the program (Figure 6.55). The utilization of the general tap will be essential, as billing information is contained within the general tab under the "billing" subheader.

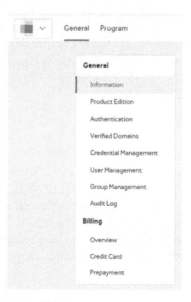

Figure 6.55 Miscellaneous program options.

6.3.1.2 Information

The information tab contains the security page information for the bug bounty program (Figure 6.56). Within this tab, program managers can name the program, assign a program handle, define the main website for the program, and write a tagline under the "About me" tab. Additionally, program managers can provide a relevant Twitter account username or update the program's logo.

Figure 6.56 Security page function.

6.3.1.3 Product Edition

HackerOne has two different product editions, the first edition is "bounty professional" and the other option is "bounty enterprise" (Figure 6.57). Program managers have the option between the two, but should consult with management and with account managers to determine the major differences and price considerations. The given price point could be a general determinant, however professional the basic edition. This tab allows program managers to see product addition statistics, and contact support for a different product.

Product Edition

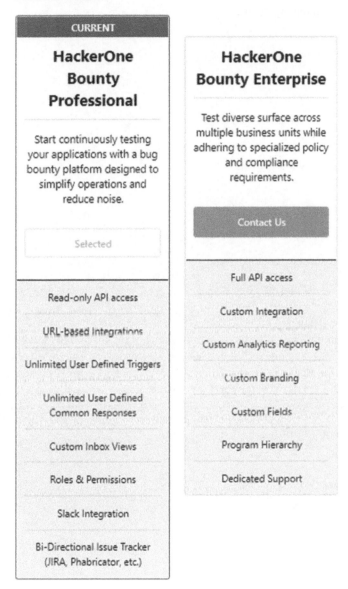

Figure 6.57 HackerOne product editions.

6.3.1.4 Authentication

Similar to Bugcrowd, HackerOne has the option to enable SSO. Program managers can click on the "Enable SAML" button. However, this is not currently shown in the screenshot example (Figure 6.58). Program managers will have to go through the IdP management team to acquire the correct settings to configure SSO. In addition, HackerOne varies from Bugcrowd as HackerOne program managers can contact their account managers to enable the IP Allowlist feature. The IP Allowlist feature will ensure that only certain IP addresses can access program management.

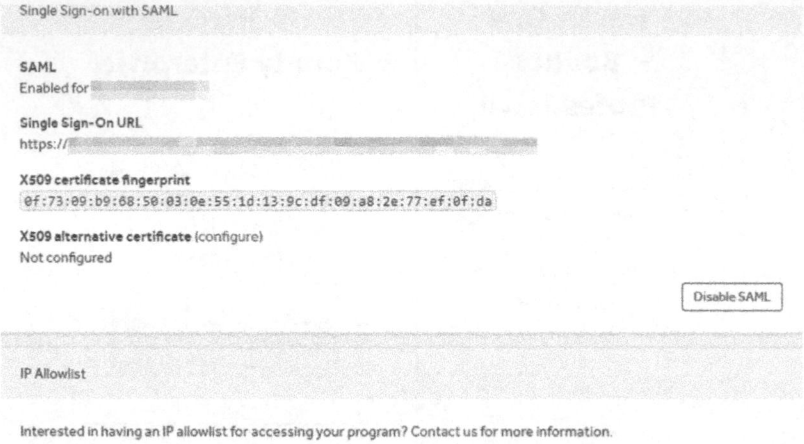

Figure 6.58   Single sign-on with SAML.

6.3.1.5   Verified Domains

The "Verify domains" tab allows a program manager to add domains, which is a requirement to enable SSO. The one difference between Bugcrowd's verification and HackerOne's verification, is that HackerOne also allows HTML meta tag verification and web file verification in addition to DNS txt records (Figure 6.59).

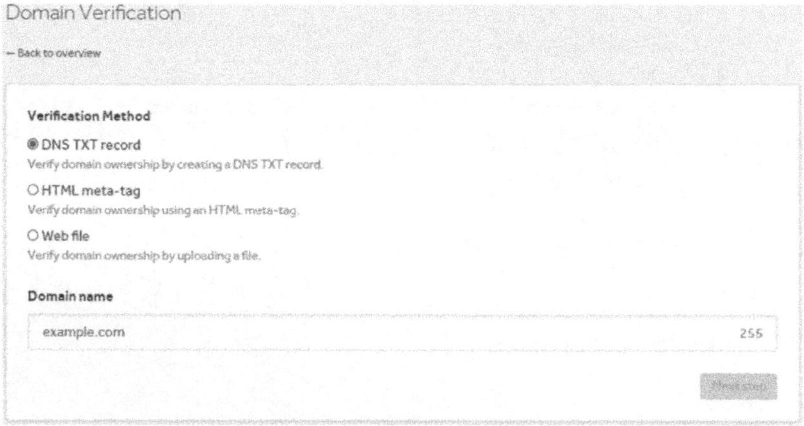

Figure 6.59   Domain verification example.

6.3.1.6 Credential Management

The "Credential management" tab allows program managers to provide CSV files to hackers in order to authenticate the application (Figure 6.60). In some cases, having an authenticated account is useful for testing for certain vulnerabilities.

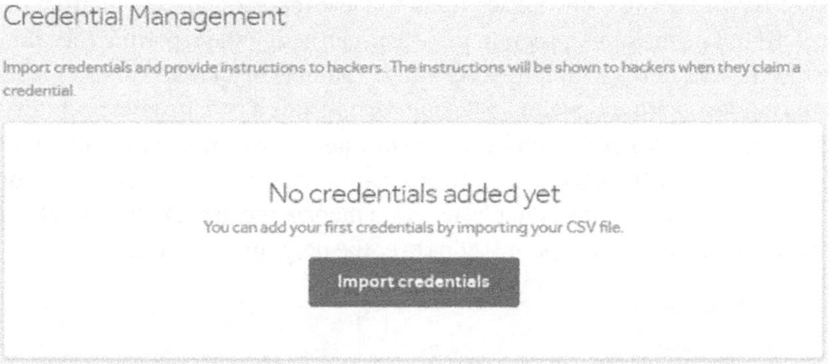

Credential Management

Import credentials and provide instructions to hackers. The instructions will be shown to hackers when they claim a credential.

No credentials added yet
You can add your first credentials by importing your CSV file.

Import credentials

Figure 6.60 Credential management tab.

6.3.1.7 Group Management

Even though user management comes before group management, setting up a group is a step that will be essential before setting up users to ensure that program managers are maintaining the best possible security practice for role-based access control, or in other words keeping their program in check. Program managers should make the best attempt to create appropriate role groups for need-to-know and essential roles. As a general rule of thumb, there should be one role that has full permissions, one role that has most permissions, and one role that has extremely limited permissions (Figure 6.61). Maintaining the

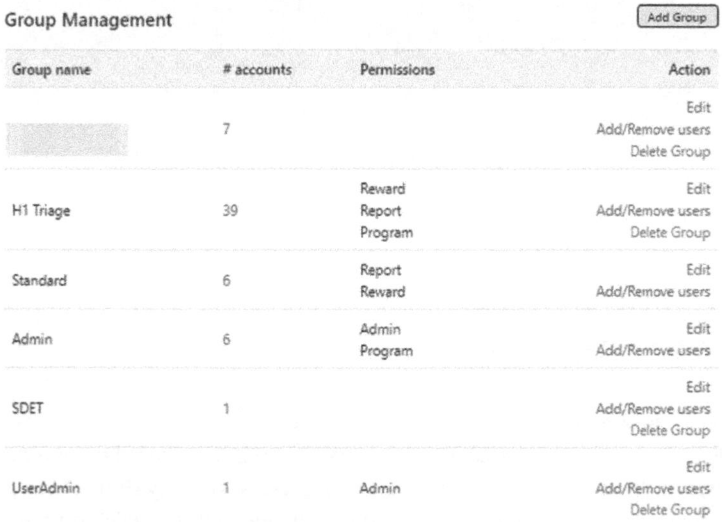

Group Management   Add Group

Group name	# accounts	Permissions	Action
	7		Edit Add/Remove users Delete Group
H1 Triage	39	Reward Report Program	Edit Add/Remove users Delete Group
Standard	6	Report Reward	Edit Add/Remove users
Admin	6	Admin Program	Edit Add/Remove users
SDET	1		Edit Add/Remove users Delete Group
UserAdmin	1	Admin	Edit Add/Remove users Delete Group

Figure 6.61 Group management options.

full suite of roles will allow program managers to assign permissions quickly without impacting the program.

To add a role group, program managers should click the "Add group" button in the top-right-hand corner of the group management pane. Once the button is clicked, the add group page will appear and program managers can name the group and assign appropriate permissions. The default level of permissions allows users to view reports and post internal comments. Outside of default permissions, program managers can assign the reporting role, the program role, the reward role, or the admin role. As a good example of a limited role, a program manager should name a group and maintain default permissions if not already set within the group management tab. Another group can be created that allows response to vulnerabilities without program management. In order to do so, program managers can assign the report role in conjunction with the reward role. Finally, program managers can click all of the checkboxes to enable others to have full admin permissions over the program (Figure 6.62).

Figure 6.62 Group management options.

6.3.1.8 User Management

Once the role groups are made, users can be added to the groups based on appropriate roles to keep the program efficient and well managed. Adding users is a fairly simple task, the only thing program managers have to do is click on the user management tab, click on the "Invite User" button, and then enter an email address and pick the groups to assign to the user (Figure 6.63).

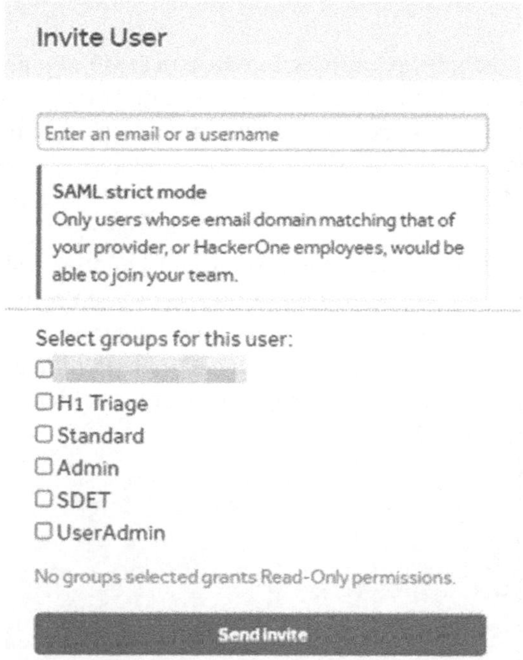

Invite User

Enter an email or a username

SAML strict mode
Only users whose email domain matching that of
your provider, or HackerOne employees, would be
able to join your team.

Select groups for this user:
☐
☐ H1 Triage
☐ Standard
☐ Admin
☐ SDET
☐ UserAdmin

No groups selected grants Read-Only permissions.

Send invite

Figure 6.63 Adding users option.

6.3.1.9 Audit Log

The final section of the general subheader is the audit log. The audit log is for viewing all
of the events that have occurred within the program (Figure 6.64). The events include
actions that team members have taken as well as user agents and the date and region of
occurrence. Maintaining accountability for actions within the program is important, especially if a lot of employees are participating in managing the program. In addition,
HackerOne allows program managers to search by event, user, or date of the event occurrence. Audit log data can also be downloaded in CSV format.

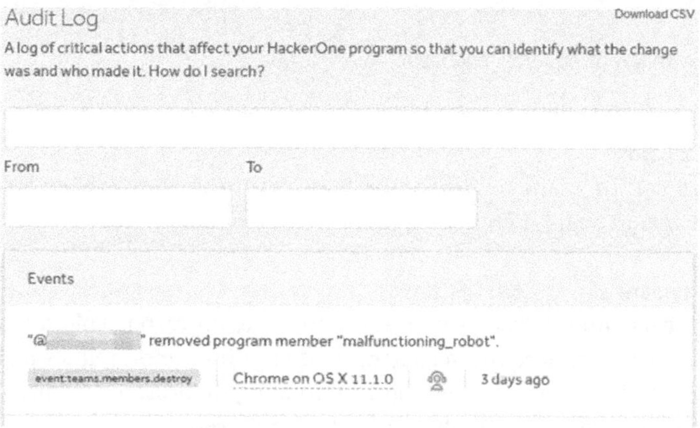

Audit Log   Download CSV

A log of critical actions that affect your HackerOne program so that you can identify what the change
was and who made it. How do I search?

From   To

Events

"@   " removed program member "malfunctioning_robot".

event.teams.members.destroy   Chrome on OS X 11.1.0   ⚙   3 days ago

Figure 6.64 Audit log option.

6.3.2 Billing

The billing subheader includes an overview, credit card setup, and prepayment for the bug bounty program pool. As stated in Section 6.3, it is essential to set up the billing section and fund the bounty pool as soon as possible. Delays in funding could result in a delay in the launch of the program.

6.3.2.1 Overview

The overview section includes the current balance of bounties and fees that a program manager has paid to security researchers. In this section, an activity report is available which allows program managers to see all of the dates that they have awarded researchers as well as the fees and running balance (Figure 6.65). Program managers can change the billing period, and view all of the month's activity history. Additionally, program managers can export reports as PDF or CSV files.

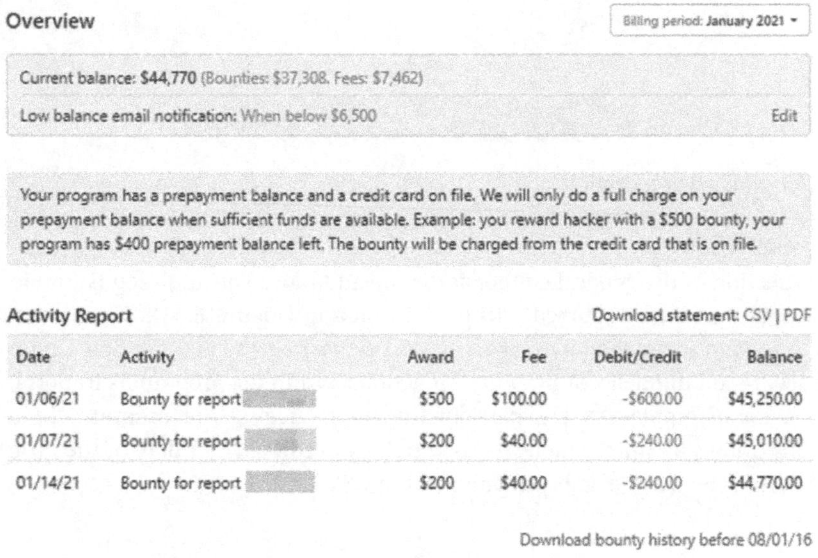

Overview

Billing period: January 2021 ▾

Current balance: **$44,770** (Bounties: $37,308. Fees: $7,462)

Low balance email notification: When below $6,500   Edit

Your program has a prepayment balance and a credit card on file. We will only do a full charge on your prepayment balance when sufficient funds are available. Example: you reward hacker with a $500 bounty, your program has $400 prepayment balance left. The bounty will be charged from the credit card that is on file.

Activity Report   Download statement: CSV | PDF

Date	Activity	Award	Fee	Debit/Credit	Balance
01/06/21	Bounty for report	$500	$100.00	-$600.00	$45,250.00
01/07/21	Bounty for report	$200	$40.00	-$240.00	$45,010.00
01/14/21	Bounty for report	$200	$40.00	-$240.00	$44,770.00

Download bounty history before 08/01/16

Figure 6.65   Overview of bounties and fees.

6.3.2.2 Credit Card

The credit card portion of the billing section is straightforward. A credit card can be saved within this section to be used for adding money to the bounty pool.

6.3.2.3 Prepayment

Program managers should consult with the finance team responsible for organizational funding, or contact their account managers to seek guidance on requesting invoices and prepayments. Specific enterprises will have internal regulations for invoices. Therefore, it is pertinent to ensure that the correct procedure is followed.

6.3.3 Program

The program subheader of the program's setting tab, is used for the majority of the technical details that will be used for configuring the program and managing hacker interactions. Program managers can depend on this tab to set up nearly every aspect of the bug bounty program. Nonetheless, bug bounty crowdsourcing platforms typically have similar options. Even with option overlap, program managers should be aware of subtle differences in configurations between platforms.

6.3.3.1 Policy

HackerOne's policy tab is nearly identical to Bugcrowd's policy configuration options. Owing to the nature of the policy being in use for a live, private bug bounty program, a screenshot will not be included. However, rest assured that the overlap makes the policy configuration within HackerOne easy to understand.

6.3.3.2 Scope

The scope configurations within HackerOne are completely different from Bugcrowd's scope and assets configuration. Program managers can click on the "Add asset" button, which will allow them to determine the rating and criticality of the assets as well as set labels, add instructions, and the live addition of the asset to the program. The "Add asset" page allows program managers to get fairly granular with considerations for researchers testing on the specific asset. In addition, program managers can scroll over most of the labels to determine what the labels mean (Figure 6.66).

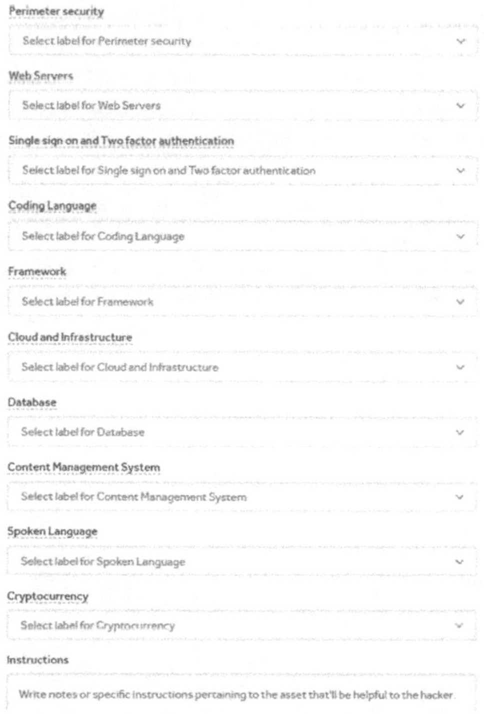

Figure 6.66 Adding assets.

To determine the environmental score of an asset, program managers must understand the CIA Triad. The CIA Triad stands for confidentiality, integrity, and availability (Figure 6.67). Confidentiality impact can be determined by the exposure of sensitive data to a threat actor. Integrity typically pertains to the modification of data. For instance, a high integrity impact rating would mean that all of the files can be modified by a threat actor. Lastly, availability is the determination of the uptime of an asset. A program manager may think of availability as an environmental factor that is only impacted by a certain suite of vulnerabilities. However, program managers must consider how a specific type of attack affects all of the environmental factors. As an example, remote code execution could result in a total loss of confidentiality, integrity, and availability. If a threat actor were to gain complete root access to a server, for instance, they could shut the server down, steal data, or modify any of the data on the server giving the vulnerability the highest rating for environmental score. Other than the difference in criticality scoring, the scope is similar to most of the other program options utilized by other platforms.

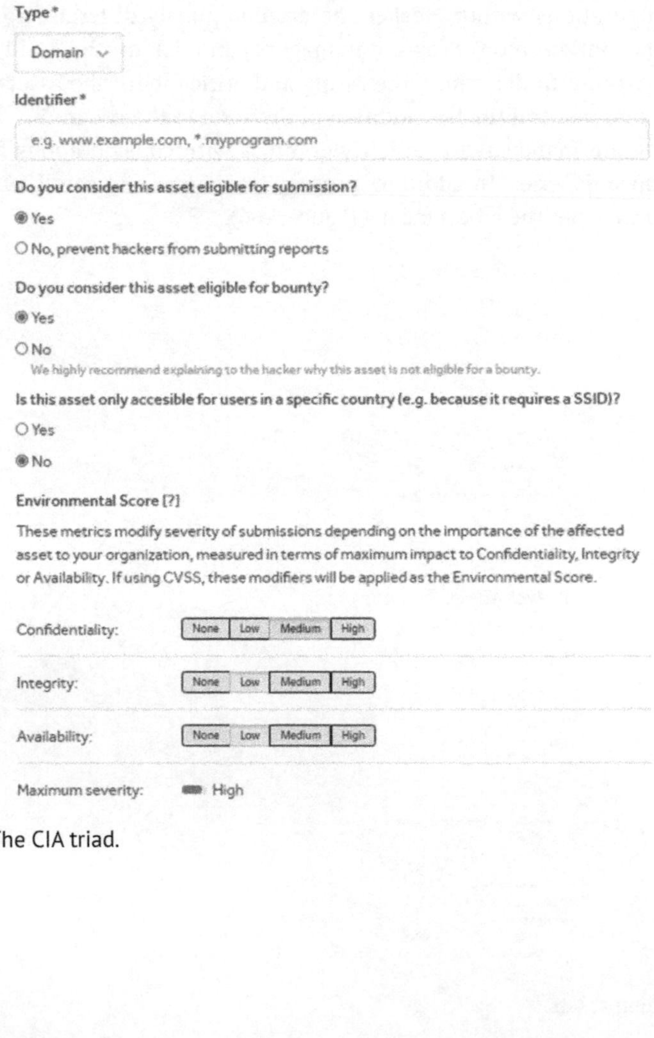

Type*

Domain ⌄

Identifier*

e.g. www.example.com, *.myprogram.com

Do you consider this asset eligible for submission?

◉ Yes

○ No, prevent hackers from submitting reports

Do you consider this asset eligible for bounty?

◉ Yes

○ No

    We highly recommend explaining to the hacker why this asset is not eligible for a bounty.

Is this asset only accesible for users in a specific country (e.g. because it requires a SSID)?

○ Yes

◉ No

Environmental Score [?]

These metrics modify severity of submissions depending on the importance of the affected asset to your organization, measured in terms of maximum impact to Confidentiality, Integrity or Availability. If using CVSS, these modifiers will be applied as the Environmental Score.

Confidentiality: | None | Low | Medium | High |

Integrity: | None | Low | Medium | High |

Availability: | None | Low | Medium | High |

Maximum severity: 🔵 High

Figure 6.67 The CIA triad.

6.3.3.3 Submit Report Form

The "Submit Report Form" tab is where program managers can customize the introduction for submission templates (Figure 6.68). Program managers can customize the submit report form even allowing or hiding specific weakness configurations (Figure 6.69). However, it is highly recommended that program managers only hide weakness

Figure 6.68 Submit report form option.

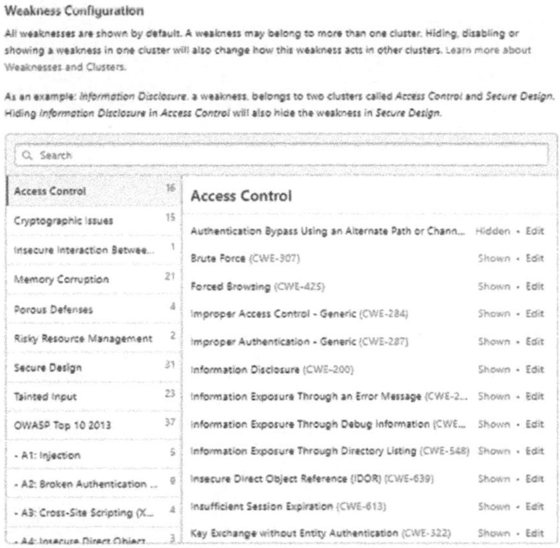

Figure 6.69 Customizing the report form.

configurations that are blatantly regarded as out-of-scope attack vectors. Program managers should not attempt to hide legitimate weakness configurations just because they do not want to deal with the report. If the vulnerability is a legitimate issue, it would be better for the security posture of the enterprise if the program allows the submission and resolves appropriately.

6.3.3.4 Response Targets

The "Response Targets" tab is where the program manager can set the time to "first response but time to triage" and the time to bounty as a baseline for the program (Figure 6.70). Additionally, the time to resolution projection can also be set for each vulnerability pending on the corresponding criticality. All of the days that the program manager sets as a target are just that: an anticipated date of action and not necessarily representative of the actual time it will take. Also, the target dates per action or in business days means that weekends do not count or identified the days the enterprise does not operate. An important aspect of evaluating the response targets is being honest as a program manager. While setting up the bug bounty program, the configuration should not be set to unrealistic response targets as it will dissuade researchers from future participation, especially if the targets are consistently missed.

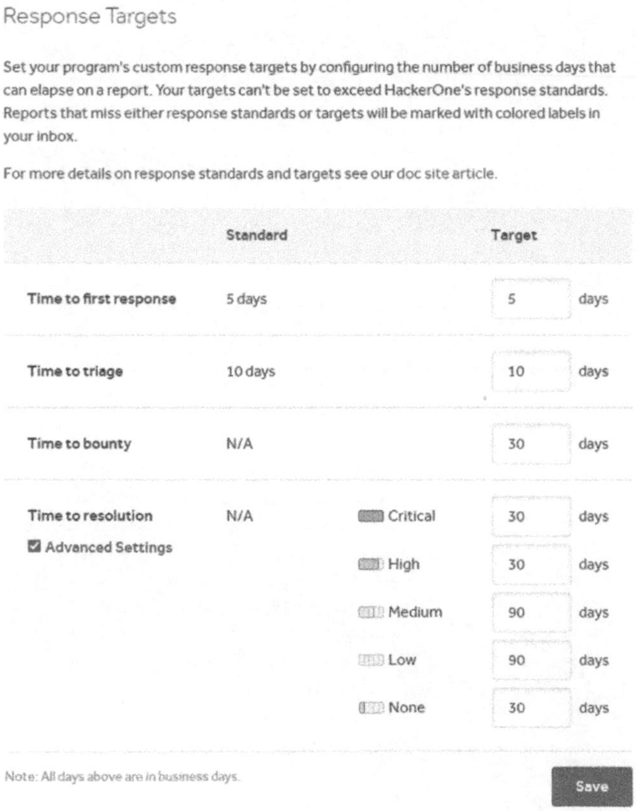

Response Targets

Set your program's custom response targets by configuring the number of business days that can elapse on a report. Your targets can't be set to exceed HackerOne's response standards. Reports that miss either response standards or targets will be marked with colored labels in your inbox.

For more details on response standards and targets see our doc site article.

	Standard		Target	
Time to first response	5 days		5	days
Time to triage	10 days		10	days
Time to bounty	N/A		30	days
Time to resolution ☑ Advanced Settings	N/A	Critical	30	days
		High	30	days
		Medium	90	days
		Low	90	days
		None	30	days

Note: All days above are in business days.

Save

Figure 6.70 Response targets option.

It is not of the highest priority to get the exact target days to resolve correctly. However, program managers should aspire to uphold the timelines they set out between response, triage, bounty, and resolution. If a program manager runs a bug bounty program for a long time. They are likely to eventually miss a target. Nonetheless, program managers should not take this too hard, but rather should learn from their mistakes.

6.3.3.5 Metrics Display

The metrics display tab shows various statistics that could potentially attract security researchers to the bug bounty program (Figure 6.71). However, the metrics that are displayed are completely up to the program manager. There isn't necessarily a "wrong" way to display metrics.

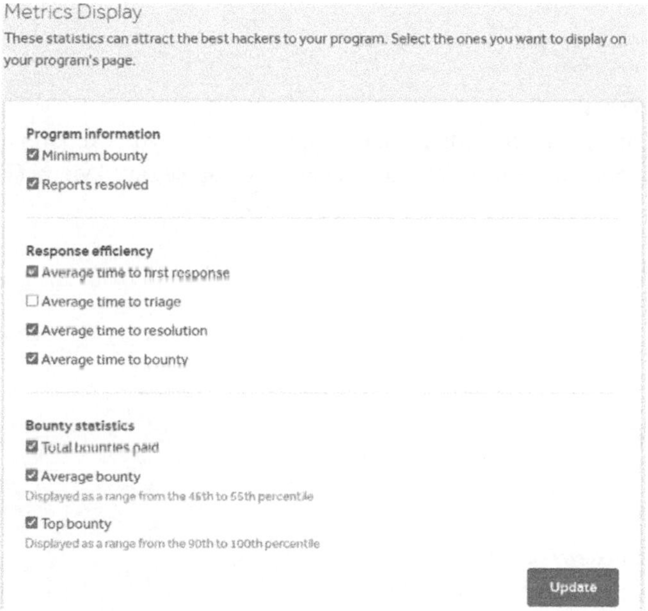

Figure 6.71 Metrics display option.

6.3.3.6 Email Notifications

The email notifications tab is self-explanatory. Program managers have the ability to choose from three options. The options given are "No content," "Minimal content," and "Full content" (Figure 6.72).

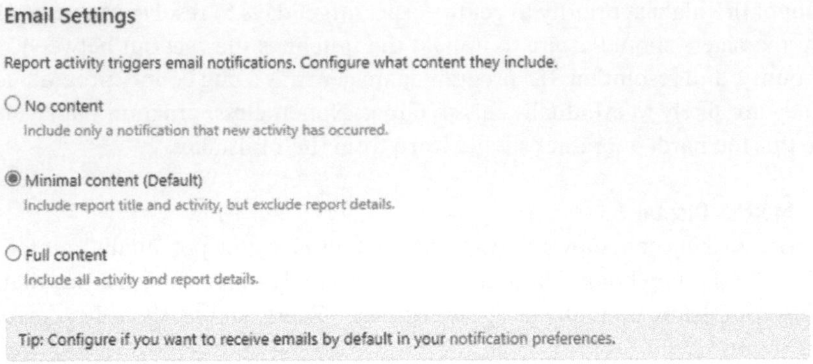

Email Settings

Report activity triggers email notifications. Configure what content they include.

○ No content
   Include only a notification that new activity has occurred.

◉ Minimal content (Default)
   Include report title and activity, but exclude report details.

○ Full content
   Include all activity and report details.

Tip: Configure if you want to receive emails by default in your notification preferences.

Figure 6.72   Setting email notifications.

6.3.3.7   Inbox Views

In short, these are quick views that can execute filters applied to reports in the inbox tab. Program managers can come to this tab to enable or disable saved views (Figure 6.73).

Inbox Views

Show, hide, rearrange or remove views below. To save a new view, go to your Inbox, select your filters, then click "Save".

View name	
☰ New & Unassigned	Shown • Remove
☰ H1 Triage	Shown • Remove

Figure 6.73   Inbox views option.

6.3.3.8   Disclosure

Enabling this function allows hackers to disclose reports in the program (Figure 6.74).

Allow hackers to disclose reports in your private program   ( ) NO

Figure 6.74   Disclosure option.

6.3.3.9   Custom Fields

The "Custom Fields" tab allows a program manager to tag reports with key value data. Unfortunately, this feature is only available to enterprise edition users. Bugcrowd, on the other hand, includes this functionality by default.

6.3.3.10 Invitations

Hacker invitations are just that: a functionality that is utilized to invite hackers to the program. This tab allows the invitation by email, username, or reputation. In addition, a report volume can be set; the report volume allows program managers to set a minimum report desire (Figure 6.75). If the minimum is not met, the program will automatically invite hackers until the number of monthly reports is met.

Invitations

☑ **Ready to open your program to the public?**
Consider a public launch.

Enable HackerOne to manage your hacker invitations so that you can ensure engagement of hackers and meet your target report volume. We steadily issue invitations to hackers who meet the following criteria within the last 90 days:

- Established reputation
- Positive signal
- Clear record with zero code of conduct violations

Report volume [?]
If this is set to 0, no invites will be sent for your program. We recommend starting out your report volume with 5 valid reports. Learn more here   [5]   [Save]

Manually invite a hacker by email, username or reputation

Invited Hackers (95)

Figure 6.75 Invitations option.

When program managers are ready for a public launch, this is where they can go to launch the incentive (Figure 6.76). HackerOne recommends that the program contains at least 100 hackers before launching to the public. Additionally, HackerOne warns that a bug bounty program can receive up to 200 reports in the first week of going public and that reverting back to private can affect the program and hackers negatively.

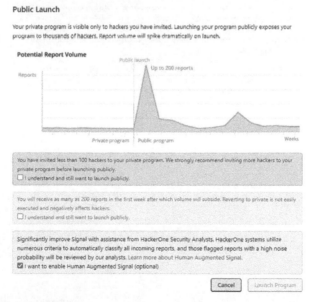

Public Launch

Your private program is visible only to hackers you have invited. Launching your program publicly exposes your program to thousands of hackers. Report volume will spike dramatically on launch.

Potential Report Volume

You have invited less than 100 hackers to your private program. We strongly recommend inviting more hackers to your private program before launching publicly.
☐ I understand and still want to launch publicly.

You will receive as many as 200 reports in the first week after which volume will subside. Reverting to private is not easily executed and negatively affects hackers.
☐ I understand and still want to launch publicly.

Significantly improve Signal with assistance from HackerOne Security Analysts. HackerOne systems utilize numerous criteria to automatically classify all incoming reports, and those flagged reports with a high noise probability will be reviewed by our analysts. Learn more about Human Augmented Signal.
☑ I want to enable Human Augmented Signal (optional)

[Cancel] [Launch Program]

Figure 6.76 Public launch option.

6.3.3.11 Submission

The submission tab utilizes the ability to limit who has access to the program by creating signal restrictions that affect how many reports can be submitted (Figure 6.77). Four different settings allow security researchers to submit more or fewer reports. For example, a strict signal setting would be the best option for a new bug bounty program, especially if the program manager doesn't have much experience with bug bounty programs. However, conversely, turning off signal requirements are for the most seasoned of bug bounty programs. Usually, choosing the standard signal option is best practice.

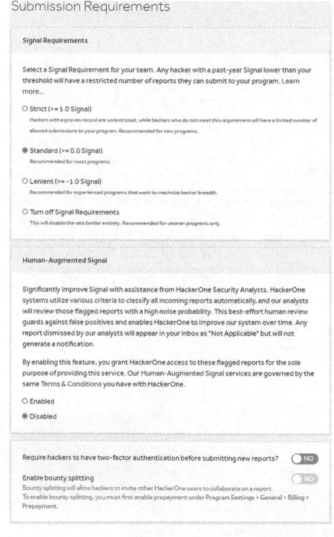

Figure 6.77 Submission requirements option.

Additionally, enabling "Human-augmented Signal" will allow HackerOne permission to allow analysts from HackerOne to classify all incoming reports. This human review could be a good feature to enable as it can assist in preventing spam or bad reports. However, the feature should be used with caution. If the report is rejected, it will be marked as "Not Applicable" but will not generate a notification for the bug bounty program. A lack of a generated notification could potentially be bad for a program manager new to bug bounty programs, especially if mistakes are made in the flagging process.

The last part of the submission section allows a forced requirement of two-factor authentication and bounty splitting. While there may be legitimate concern for some programs, it's not an absolute necessity to force hackers to have two-factor authentication and may actually discourage program participation. Bounty splitting is an essential feature if the enterprise can afford to set up prepayment for programs. Encouraging hacker collaboration and participation can lead to more unique, critical exploits that are presented to the organization.

6.3.3.12 Message Hackers

The ability to message hackers is yet another standard feature offered by most bug bounty program platforms. HackerOne's functionality specifically allows program managers to select specific groups of security researchers to message (Figure 6.78).

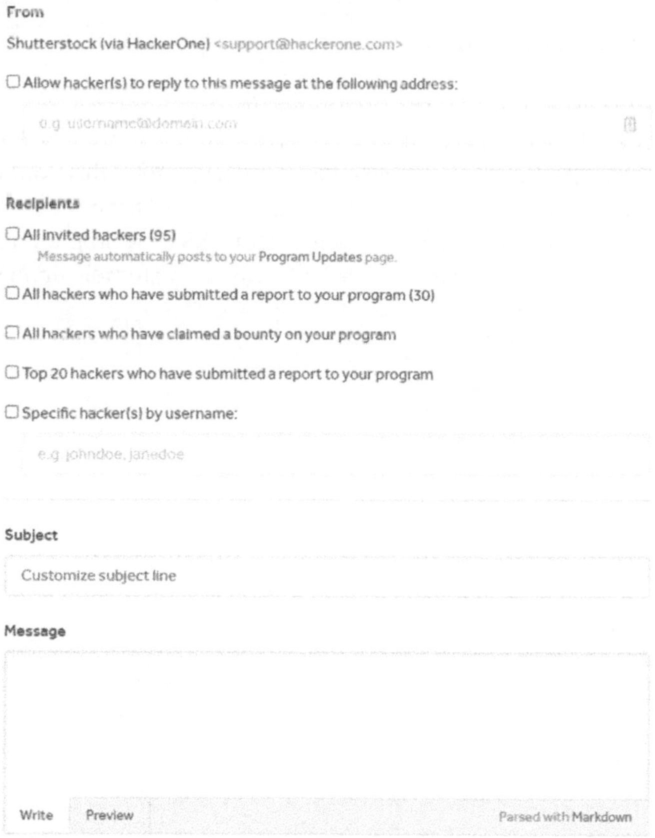

From

Shutterstock (via HackerOne) <support@hackerone.com>

☐ Allow hacker(s) to reply to this message at the following address:

> e.g. username@domain.com

Recipients

☐ All invited hackers (95)
> Message automatically posts to your Program Updates page.

☐ All hackers who have submitted a report to your program (30)

☐ All hackers who have claimed a bounty on your program

☐ Top 20 hackers who have submitted a report to your program

☐ Specific hacker(s) by username:

> e.g. johndoe, janedoe

Subject

> Customize subject line

Message

Write   Preview   Parsed with Markdown

Figure 6.78 Messaging hackers option.

6.3.3.13 Email Forwarding

The ability to set up an email address and enable email forwarding allows program managers to receive relevant vulnerability reports (Figure 6.79). Enabling this functionality is helpful in the event that an enterprise wants to keep its bug bounty program somewhat private. Providing a good forwarding email on a security page or security.txt could prove useful. Programs will receive these emails in the HackerOne inbox. However, one should note that this could create spam too. Therefore, a dedicated email for the HackerOne program is recommended.

Figure 6.79 Email forwarding function.

6.3.3.14 Embedded Submission Form

First and foremost, the embedded submission form option is only available to enterprises that have the Enterprise edition of HackerOne. Unfortunately, this could not be tested, because of my product model. However, the form appears to have the same functionality that comes with Bugcrowd's program natively (Figure 6.80). A program manager can set up and embed the form on a web page for hackers who may stumble upon vulnerabilities.

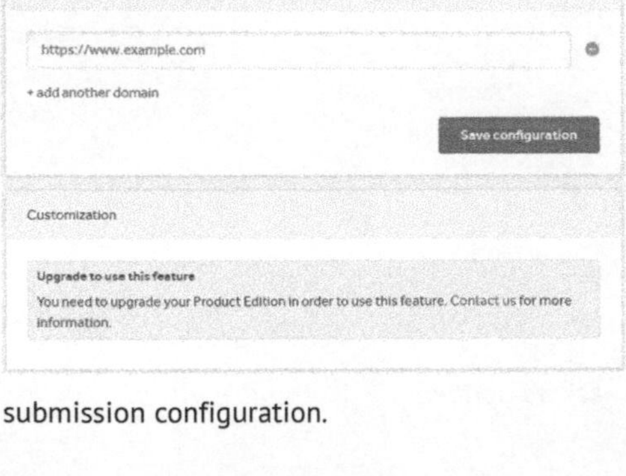

Figure 6.80 Embedded submission configuration.

6.3.3.15 Bounties

Rewarding researchers is the bread and butter of a bug bounty program. Within HackerOne's "Bounties" tab, there are several things that can be done (Figure 6.81). For one, specific monetary reward values can be assigned per asset. In addition, custom bounty headings can be made or other rows can be inserted. It's *not* recommended to make up custom criticality ratings, as this can be confusing to hackers who have previously utilized the standard low/medium/high/critical ratings. The optional description field allows program managers to discuss the specifics of rewards and, underneath, a history of bounties that were paid out can be seen.

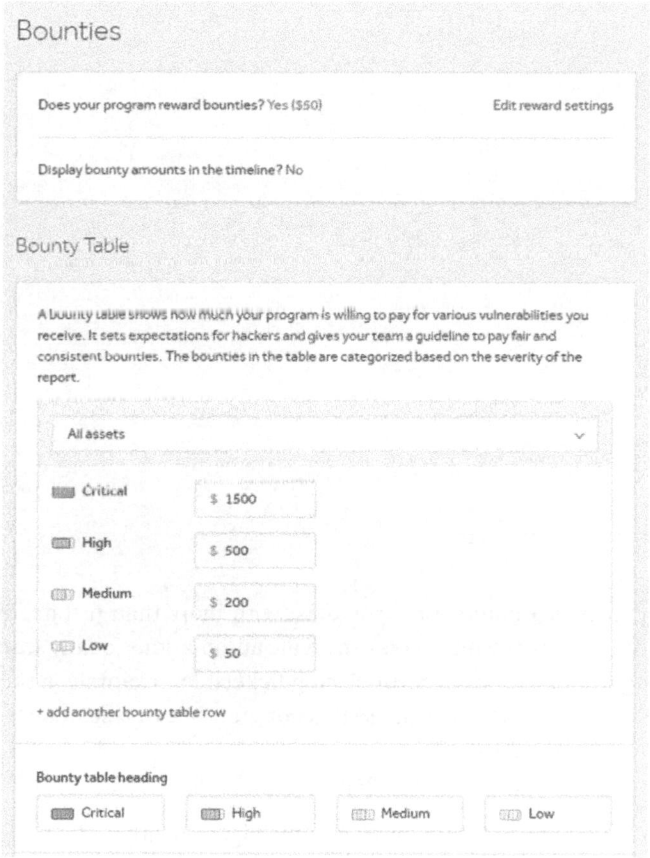

Figure 6.81 Bounties option.

6.3.3.16 Swag

Within this tab, there isn't much to cover. An option to turn swag awards on or off is available. If you don't know what swag is, it's basically company-branded apparel or items that programs can opt to give out to hackers for participating in the program.

6.3.3.17 Common Responses

When managing a bug bounty program, enterprises will find an annoyance in out-of-scope or nonvulnerable/unqualifying vulnerability reports. The "Common responses" tab provides an easy way for program managers to add custom responses to mitigate considerable nonissues that are reported to the program (Figure 6.82).

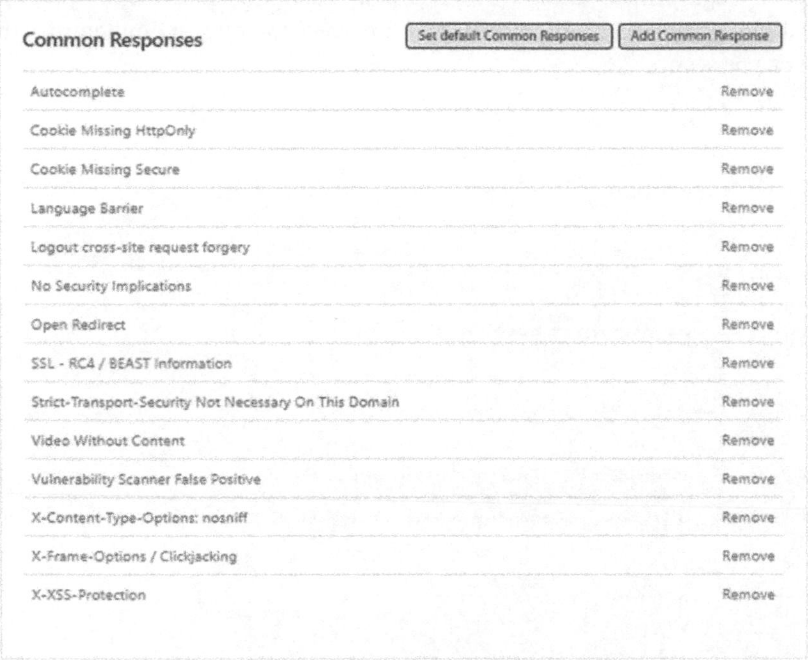

Common Responses	Set default Common Responses	Add Common Response
Autocomplete		Remove
Cookie Missing HttpOnly		Remove
Cookie Missing Secure		Remove
Language Barrier		Remove
Logout cross-site request forgery		Remove
No Security Implications		Remove
Open Redirect		Remove
SSL - RC4 / BEAST Information		Remove
Strict-Transport-Security Not Necessary On This Domain		Remove
Video Without Content		Remove
Vulnerability Scanner False Positive		Remove
X-Content-Type-Options: nosniff		Remove
X-Frame-Options / Clickjacking		Remove
X-XSS-Protection		Remove

Figure 6.82 Common reponses option.

The common responses automation can assist with more than just dealing with out-of-scope vulnerabilities. Program managers can create automations for any scenario, including a ticket changing from open to triage, or closing tickets. For example, a program manager may want to automate a common response that congratulates a researcher for participating when they are rewarded, and so on.

To create a flow, follow the following steps.

1. Click on the "Add Common Response" button (Figure 6.83):

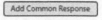

Figure 6.83 Add common response option.

2. Create the flow, set the title to something that can be remembered. As an example it could be a decent idea to title a common response as "Reward Response," and in the message field a program manager can type a message to send to a hacker after rewarding them, such as "Thank you for participating in our program! We encourage you to keep hacking!" or whatever seems like a good fit (Figure 6.84).

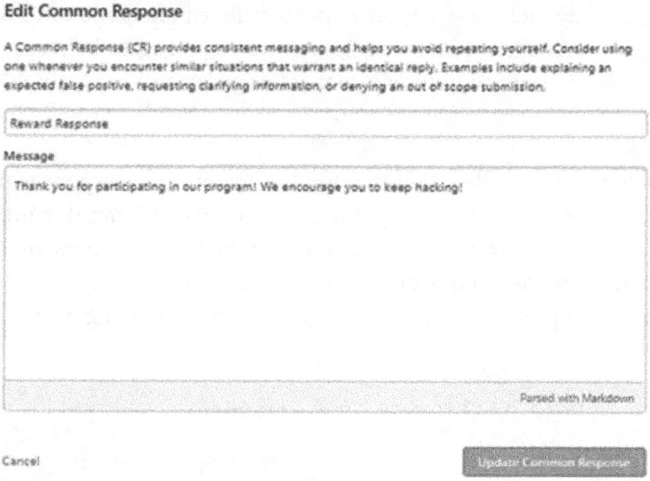

Edit Common Response
A Common Response (CR) provides consistent messaging and helps you avoid repeating yourself. Consider using one whenever you encounter similar situations that warrant an identical reply. Examples include explaining an expected false positive, requesting clarifying information, or denying an out of scope submission.
Reward Response
Message
Thank you for participating in our program! We encourage you to keep hacking!
Parsed with Markdown
Cancel
Update Common Response

Figure 6.84 Edit common response option.

3. Once the response is saved, a program manager can click on the "Default Common Responses" button to set a common response to an action (Figure 6.85):

Default Common Responses
You can use the form below to choose a default Common Response that will be used when you select an action for a report.
Change State
Triaged
none
Needs more info
none
New
none
Close Report
Resolved
none
Informative
none
Not applicable
none
Duplicate
none
Spam
none
Set Bounty
Award bounty
Reward Response
Ineligible for bounty
none
Save

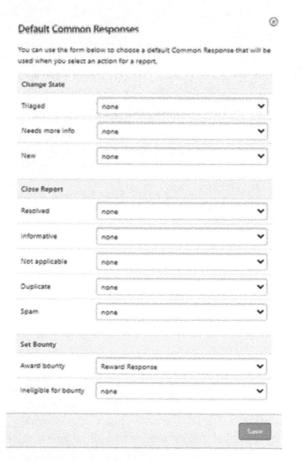

Figure 6.85 Default common responses option.

As seen, nearly any ticketing action can be utilized in conjunction with common responses. Program managers can creative baseline responses to help assist in day-to-day workflows, but it isn't a requirement of a successful program.

6.3.3.18 Triggers

The "Triggers" tab offers similar functionality to the common responses tab. However, it offers more specific wording and tuning. Enterprises can configure default rules that elicit specific responses when keywords or fields are matched. The triggers are written as basic if/then statements. Program managers can combine a wide variety of options, even multiple options to make up the various triggers. Observe the following example (Figure 6.86):

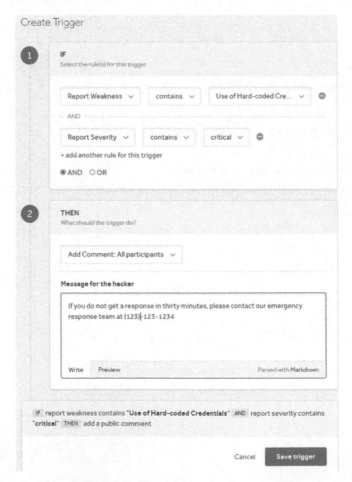

Figure 6.86 Create triggers option.

The above is broken into simple statements, and two rules were added to show how it can be utilized. First, a program manager must select what their triggering event is. So, in this instance, if the report weakness contains a use of hard-coded credentials, and the report severity contains critical, then a comment will be added to all participants in the program (bug bounty program managers and hackers) stating, "If you do not get a response in thirty minutes, please contact our emergency response team at 123-123-1234." There are many ways in which triggers can be used to increase the effectiveness of programs.

6.3.3.19 Integrations

In all, the HackerOne program options allow for more integrations than Bugcrowd. Additionally, similar to Bugcrowd, documentation for the integrations exist and can be utilized as a means of understanding the ins and outs of configuration. Again, as there are a lot of options and some are fairly specific, they are not discussed individually in this chapter.

6.3.3.20 Api

The API settings are straightforward and are also identical in many senses to Bugcrowd's API features.

6.3.3.21 Hackbot

Settings within the "Hackbot" tab enable the automation of specific actions and triggers within the bug bounty program. For the most part, all of the various settings are concise and program managers can decide what level of option functionality makes sense for their situation (Figure 6.87).

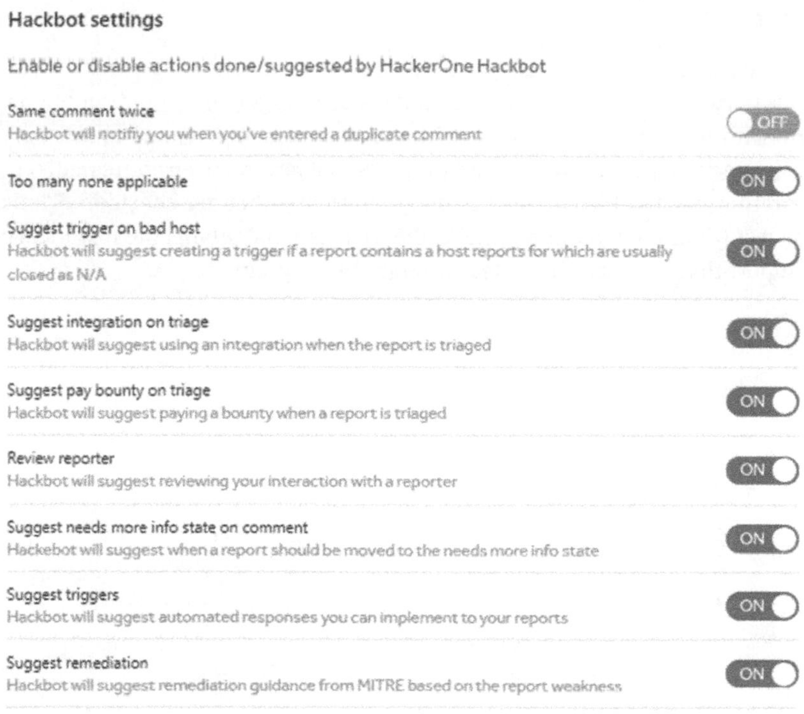

Hackbot settings

Enable or disable actions done/suggested by HackerOne Hackbot

Same comment twice
Hackbot will notifiy you when you've entered a duplicate comment — OFF

Too many none applicable — ON

Suggest trigger on bad host
Hackbot will suggest creating a trigger if a report contains a host reports for which are usually closed as N/A — ON

Suggest integration on triage
Hackbot will suggest using an integration when the report is triaged — ON

Suggest pay bounty on triage
Hackbot will suggest paying a bounty when a report is triaged — ON

Review reporter
Hackbot will suggest reviewing your interaction with a reporter — ON

Suggest needs more info state on comment
Hackebot will suggest when a report should be moved to the needs more info state — ON

Suggest triggers
Hackbot will suggest automated responses you can implement to your reports — ON

Suggest remediation
Hackbot will suggest remediation guidance from MITRE based on the report weakness — ON

Figure 6.87 Hackbot settings option.

6.3.3.22 Export Reports

The ability to export reports is simple. A program manager only has to enter in their email and all of the reports will be emailed to them (Figure 6.88). All of the vulnerability reports will take some time to process, and then when it's done the reports will be available for download as a CSV file.

Figure 6.88 Export reports option.

6.3.3.23 Profile Settings

The profile settings page is fairly standard and all in all isn't much different from other configurations. HackerOne is a little bit more unique in the sense that it blends researcher and program manager preferences together.

6.3.4 Inbox

Program managers will spend the majority of their time within the inbox, working on resolving reported vulnerabilities. The left-hand side of Figure 6.89 represents a preview of all reports within the program, starting with the new and unassigned reports. Several tabs exist for filtering reports, primarily by new reports that haven't been addressed, reports that need resolution, reports that need retesting, and reports that are considered "missed targets." The last tab of the top inbox panel is the "All" tab. It contains the historical contents of every report that has been submitted through the program.

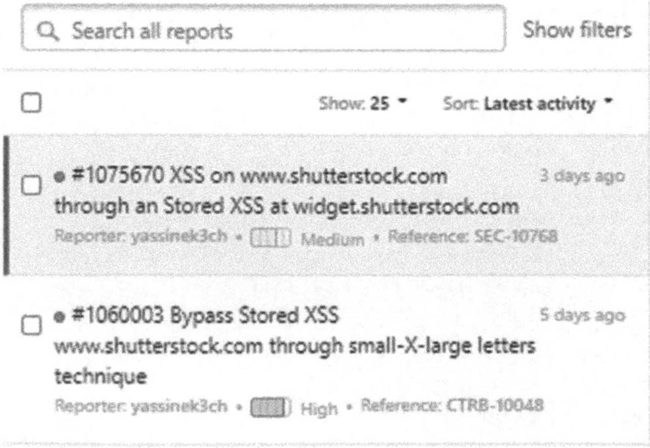

Figure 6.89 Reporting inbox vulnerabilities.

An example report is shown in Figure 6.90.

Figure 6.90 Example report.

6.3.4.1 Report Details

The fields that the report contains will change based on the platform that a program manager uses. However, many pieces repeat. For example, the "State" simply defines what phase the submission is in, the "Severity" is the criticality, the "Asset" is what the hacker is reporting on, etc.

6.3.4.2 Timeline

The portion of the report in which a hacker proves to the program that there's a legitimate proof of concept for the vulnerability is the "timeline." In short, the timeline is the overall justification including the description of the vulnerability, presumed impact caused, and the steps to replicate (Figure 6.91). The timeline is also used as a means to address any vulnerabilities that are reported. Bug bounty program managers can click on the various functions and reward hackers, add comments, close reports, etc.

Figure 6.91 Timeline option.

6.4 Summary

Creating bug bounty programs can feel complex, and while there are many options for program management platforms many of them offer similar functionality. Overall, Bugcrowd and HackerOne were used as examples, each with unique management styles and methodologies. In my opinion, Bugcrowd maintains a higher overall ease of access, setup, and program management segmentation, whereas HackerOne has more automation, filtering, and features for an exceedingly large program. Nonetheless, program managers should still research all of the options as, periodically, functionality changes.

Part 4

Vulnerability Reports and Disclosure

7

Triage and Bug Management

7.1 Understanding Triage

Triage is the act of reviewing vulnerabilities, and determining whether the report warrants further action within the intake process.

1. Determine if the asset is in scope.
   If it's not in scope, assess the criticality of the vulnerability. If it isn't a serious vulnerability, determine if the bug will be triaged. In most cases, program managers will want to triage serious bugs, even if the vulnerability is considered out of scope.
2. Analyze the report.
   This includes attempting to see if the proof of concept that was submitted is valid, determining criticality, and so on.
3. Request additional information.
   Generally speaking, a program manager should not triage a vulnerability unless it meets all of the criteria set out in the in-scope section of the program description.
   Ensure that any questionable information that's provided is clarified upon, generally, as it pertains to vulnerability validation. The criticality of the bug can be changed later in the resolution process, as well as other detail determinations.
4. Triage the bug.

7.1.1 Validation

The vulnerability validation process should be handled diligently with respect to the production environment, research authenticity, and program definitions. While this sounds complex, it translates to making sure that bug handling occurs in a way that isn't detrimental to any sort of current production processes and that adequate time and effort is dedicated to validating the bug.

In addition to ensuring that a researcher's report is handled swiftly in the validation process, programs must be diligent about validation – for their own protection in the communication processes and against financial manipulation.

Corporate Cybersecurity: Identifying Risks and the Bug Bounty Program, First Edition. John Jackson.
© 2021 John Wiley & Sons, Ltd. Published 2021 by John Wiley & Sons, Ltd.

Example 1

A security researcher reports a vulnerability in which they believe an Apache server status page is leaking information, not as a direct resource request but as a result of an open redirect vulnerability. In any case, a vulnerability defined as such could be the difference between a bug rated as low or medium to an escalation to high or critical.

If the vulnerability was a result of basic client-side server misconfiguration issues, validation is simple. The program manager just has to navigate to the affected resource with "/server-status" appended at the end of the affected resource URL. Triage would occur immediately, the misconfiguration would be fixed, and both parties would be on their way.

If the triager or program manager aren't careful, they could end up paying for a perceived vulnerability that isn't actually an issue in a production environment. In a similar sense, if the exact scenario were altered slightly and, for the sake of the example, not just a simple server misconfiguration but an SSRF (server-side request forgery), the validation process would have to be different.

As an example, a program manager may find that, because of an open redirect parameter, the researcher attempts an SSRF by using the payload http://127.0.0.1/server-status and they see the result. Upon reporting the perceived vulnerability, it appears valid. The program manager believes that the server-status page cannot be seen from the root domain, and it's confirmed that it can't be, which is indicative of an SSRF as stated. The vulnerability is initially triaged post-validation, and the program manager submits a ticket for a fix to the appropriate software engineering team.

The team states that they are unable to replicate the vulnerability. What changed? The program manager and software engineers collaborate. The software engineer cannot replicate through the same processes, yet the program manager is clearly having an issue. With a little bit of digging and investigation, it's determined that the issue isn't replicable or deemed an SSRF. In reality, the open redirect on the URL's parameter resulted in a redirect to a server that was hosted on the attacker's machine, or in other words the attacker isn't seeing an Apache server status page hosted on the enterprise end: they are seeing their own HTTP Server's status page. An accident such as this can happen, especially if the program manager frequently utilizes Linux and may inadvertently host an Apache server without knowing.

The program manager asks one of the software engineers what other ports are open for testing. One of the software engineers relays the open ports to the bug bounty program manager and the program manager tests a new SSRF payload (http://127.0.0.1:3306). There's no indication that port enumeration can be done. The program manager continues the port testing process, and gets to port 22. This time the SSRF appears to trigger. However, looking at the response in Burp Suite, the secure shell (SSH) version is completely different from what the SSH services on the enterprise backend is. After a quick check, the program manager notes that the SSH version that is being seen in the perceived SSRF lines up with the SSH version running on their host machine.

The situation: there's no SSRF vulnerability to fix because the vulnerability isn't truly an SSRF: it's only an open redirect vulnerability. The GET request is simply pulling the results from services being hosted on the client's end, basically a true redirect (with no association to enterprise assets).

7.1.2 Lessons Learned

Failure to validate and understand vulnerabilities can prove deadly for an organization. The impact can be monetary loss, software engineering distrust, and general reputational damage. It's better to take a little time to be valuable and assess the true impact of the vulnerability, and then to quickly triage it. As a note, it never hurts to coordinate with peers if the impact of the vulnerability is misunderstood or if there's any sign of strange validation anomalies. Additionally, the triage evaluation stage is a perfect time to ask a researcher for more information. Bug bounty program managers must make use of additional information gathering where necessary.

7.1.3 Vulnerability Mishaps

When vulnerability mishaps occur, it's the responsibility of the program managers to accept the mistakes. Confrontation with the security researcher over mishaps or any requests or threats made in an attempt to retrieve the money are out of bounds. At the end of the day, it's not the researcher's fault when a program does not validate the vulnerability. In fact, we are all human and it's not improbable that triage, the program manager, and the researcher could have all made a mistake. Part of growth is accepting the issue and being transparent with leadership if asked about the situation.

There's a lot of room for improvement in a program. Even the experts in the application security field know that there's no possible way they will know everything. Security is dynamic and a team effort. One of the best ways to prevent mistakes from happening again is to ensure that records of accidents have been maintained. Mishaps aren't the end of the world, but it's difficult to know what to avoid in the future if accountability for the mistakes isn't accepted.

On top of self-accountability, there's a possibility a researcher might hold themselves accountable and message the program about the mistake. Even though the probability of a researcher doing so is significantly lower, don't accept any sort of return and thank them for their honesty. No one should be punished for a mistake that was made in good faith.

7.1.4 Managed Services

Managed services are discussed in Chapter 3. It's undeniable that using managed services is an essential component for a wide range of programs. However, what does the vulnerability triage process look like in the instance that an enterprise's program managers allow a bug bounty platform to do so? Having a team of professionals makes a world of a difference when a program is bogged down with other cybersecurity incentives, and the ability to have someone validate a bug and give the researcher peace of mind is priceless.

In many cases, the program manager may wake up in the morning, log in, and find that a vulnerability is nicely triaged, and the triage team has exercised the liberty of cleaning up the researcher's report so that the program manager can adequately and quickly reproduce. Arguably, managed services can even help reduce friction in the reporting process. Both small and large enterprises can benefit in multiple ways. For example, a large program may need a dedicated triage team through managed services because the alternative might be having to hire employees to manage the program at a rate that is significantly higher than using a bug bounty platform's services. Alternatively, fewer employees can be hired for the triage process, and the current program managers can expand the program to focus on the validation portion of the reporting process. Smaller programs can typically get away with avoiding managed services, but arguably, the inexpensive nature and value of complex vulnerability validation can help smaller enterprises expand their security teams without spending too much time stuck in the triage loop.

Nonetheless, the same objective of validation must occur, whether the program includes managed services or not. We are all prone to error. If triage validates a bug, and assigns it to the program for resolution, revalidate and ensure it meets scope criteria

7.1.5 Self-service

The process of managing one's own process from report to end isn't impossible or improbable. When an enterprise chooses to do so, it's safe to say that the triage and validation portions of the report can nearly be combined. However, program managers should be aware of the importance of separating triage or validation and impact assessments. Vulnerabilities should not be automatically triaged unless program managers are absolutely certain that it is a vulnerability and that there's no question about it. If the vulnerability can wait, triage should always have a first look because a second opinion is a far safer option.

7.2 Bug Management

The entire report management process can take quite a bit of preparation and understanding to turn a clunky process into a smooth workflow. Even though every aspect of the process is important, the overall vulnerability management portion is the portion that the enterprise cares about above all else – it is the reason why the program exists in the first place. Try not to have a negative mentality or stress about the bug management process. Application security engineers are typically equipped to deal with bug bounty programs more effectively because of their experience in the software development lifecycle (SDLC), but realistically any cybersecurity engineer can manage this process with the right organizational setup.

7.2.1 Vulnerability Priority

Even though triage is responsible for the initial intake and validation of specific reports, it's not their job to prioritize the vulnerabilities internally. A common misconception within program management is the taxonomy of triaged items. For the most part, vulnerabilities are accurately rated within the reporting processes. Nonetheless, a program manager should be careful not to use vulnerability taxonomy as something set in stone.

For example, please go to a search engine and look up the following CVE to evaluate: CVE-2020-14179. As it stands, this is rated as medium on the common vulnerability scoring system (CVSS) version 3.x scale. Obviously, as is known up to this point the criticality will determine the payout. The question is, what is the comparison of the CVE in the program versus the CVE in reality? Realistically, the vulnerability may be rated medium, but by reading the current description, it can be seen that it's an information disclosure vulnerability and may be on the lower end of the scale. An attacker can essentially view field names and custom service level agreement (SLA) names on Jira tickets. The vulnerability may not be too serious in retrospect. However, the CVSS score is the typical scoring mechanism for bug bounty programs. Therefore, a medium would likely have to be paid (or at least recommended). The importance of establishing bounty pay ranges instead of set values shines in this regard because the Jira vulnerability can now be paid at the lower end of the medium scale in severity. Paying on the lower end of the scale shouldn't be commonplace within a program. Program managers must always remember to stick to payout guidelines, and be fair to the researcher, especially if the vulnerability is a legitimate issue. Programs should not look for ways to pay a researcher less, but instead evaluate impact to see if a researcher should be getting paid more.

Now, compare the Jira vulnerability to a standard cross-site scripting (XSS) vulnerability. Regardless of what asset the vulnerability affects, an XSS vulnerability will always have more exploitation use cases than CVE-2020-14179, as long as it's not considered self-XSS. An information disclosure bug isn't as serious as being able to phish users and steal credentials, in nearly every circumstance (unless the information disclosure is sensitive, such as passwords, PII, etc.).

Take a look at three vulnerabilities and determine the order in which these should be resolved. Rate them on a scale between 1 and 3, where 1 is the highest priority and three is the lowest:

7.2.2 Vulnerability Examples

7.2.2.1 Reflected XSS on a login portal

Report and Triage
A researcher found a XSS vulnerability on the login portal by abusing a native parameter. They are able to pop-up alerts, and the proof used the classic <script>alert(1)</script> technique. The alert is triaged by managed services as a medium rated vulnerability.

Validation
The program is able to validate the vulnerability as a legitimate XSS vulnerability.

7.2.2.2 Open redirect vulnerability

Report and Triage
The same researcher finds a vulnerability that allows them to redirect users to any website, with no restrictions. Additionally, the researcher notes that they are able to check if specific ports are open and are closed on the backend with the URL "http://127.0.0.1:port" appended to the path. They reported it as an open redirection vulnerability because they are having a difficult time telling if the ports are actually opened or closed – it's just the researcher's guess. The alert is triaged by managed services as a medium rated vulnerability, as they could not validate any sort of service-side request forgery vulnerability.

Validation

The program is able to validate the open redirection vulnerability. Additionally, they've noted that the ability to enumerate internal ports and even see contents of specific files is possible through testing.

7.2.2.3   Leaked internal Structured Query Language (SQL) server credentials

Report and Triage

Lastly, a vulnerability was found in which the enterprise's public GitHub repository appears to be leaking credentials for a My Structured Query Language (MYSQL) server over port 3306. Triage is unable to validate the authenticity, as the credentials appear to be accessible from the internal subnet only.

Validation

The program validates the existence of the credentials, and has determined that the exposed internal credentials are legitimate. However, the program, in keeping with best practice, determines that this vulnerability is rated at a medium rated vulnerability.

7.3   Answers

In the three given scenarios, the results are ranked from least to most pertinent, along with an explanation of why.

7.3.1.1   Reflected XSS in a login portal

The reflected XSS vulnerability ranks below the open redirect that escalates into an SSRF. Realistically, the ease of exploitation and possibility of phishing credentials can be highly disruptive to the business and causes a lot of strife and impact in the enterprise's security process. An XSS, in most cases, ends up as a true medium unless the researcher manages to escalate the vulnerability to an instance of account takeover.

7.3.1.2   Open redirect vulnerability

While this vulnerability starts out as a low-impact, redirect based-scenario, the researcher was able to turn it into a server-side request forgery vulnerability by attempting to enumerate ports. Additionally, the program manager was able to read other files, turning a low-impact vulnerability into a high-impact vulnerability. In this instance, it would be recommended to escalate the researcher's vulnerability from a low to a high since they identified the possibility of the SSRF attack. However, this would not be considered critical, because no further escalation had occurred from the researcher's part. Resolving this issue first would be the best recommendation to prevent critical exploitation or data leakage.

7.3.1.3   Leaked internal SQL server credentials

While at first glance the internal SQL server exposure may appear to be the most critical vulnerability, if anything, it's either equally as vulnerable or less than the instance of the reflected XSS. An enterprise shouldn't sleep on a vulnerability that's considered internally reproducible only, though. In the instance legitimate internal credentials are exposed, even if the researcher cannot access them, tell the affected team to rotate the credentials immediately. A common misconception about internal credentials is that it's not problematic because a security researcher cannot get onto the network; this couldn't be further from the truth.

7.3.1 Vulnerability Rating-test Summary

The truth is, the perception of how vulnerabilities are handled has some room for flexibility, and it's impossible to set strict guidelines. What triage considers critical may only be a medium for the enterprise. If the leaked internal SQL server credentials example were for a critical asset such as a database that held credit cards, or PII, would the priority change? Understanding that the taxonomy and priority of vulnerability remediation may change/have to change is an essential part of program management.

7.3.2 Complexity vs Rating

No one can thoroughly define how the enterprise should manage different vulnerabilities. Generally, there's a baseline. But as we've seen, a baseline is just that: an outline of a recommended approach. Alternatively, a good way to address various issues is to compare all of the factors, starting with the complexity of the vulnerability and the rating.

- **Complexity**: how difficult replicating a vulnerability is, with respect to how difficult the vulnerability would be to replicate by an unskilled threat actor. Imagine that the rating scale ranges from very easy, to easy, medium, hard, extremely hard.
- **Rating**: the severity or impact of a vulnerability that is exploited by a threat actor. The rating scale can be realistic, in one of these categories: non-applicable, informational, low, medium, high, critical.

The baseline for evaluating vulnerabilities against complexity and rating doesn't have to use strict wording, nor does it have to be included in the bug bounty program's description, or even written down. It's meant to be a mental note to keep in mind while evaluating vulnerabilities for triage priority as well as helping during the logical process of working through reported bugs when monetary ranges need to be evaluated.

To understand how the complexity and rating scales are used in conjunction with each other, note the following two separate examples and compare them.

1. Stack based buffer overflow on example.exe resulting in remote code execution.

A vulnerability was identified in which it were possible to perform a buffer overflow exploit against the example.exe file offered by company.com.

2. Local file inclusion (LFI) vulnerability led to remote file inclusion (RFI) resulting in remote code execution.

A vulnerability was identified in which the foo.php?page = parameter suffered from a local file inclusion vulnerability. When a payload of ../../../../../../etc/passwd was appended to the end of the parameter, the vulnerability was exploited. Additionally, swapping out the LFI payload with a PHP input wrapper (php://input) and modifying POST request data to include <? system('uname -a'); ?> resulted in full remote code execution on the system.

7.3.3 Projected Ratings

Example 2

Complexity: hard. An unskilled threat actor would have a difficult time performing a stack based buffer overflow if public scripts don't exist for it.

Rating: critical. Remote code execution can give a threat actor full control over an asset.

Example 3

Complexity: medium. An unskilled threat actor could stumble upon this vulnerability with a little bit of targeted fuzzing. Multiple scripts and methodologies exist for abusing the vulnerability. However, fuzzing and scripting may only get the threat actor so far. Therefore, it's not rated as very easy.

Rating: high/critical. The vulnerability within itself may be rated as a critical overall, but the initial starting point of the bug would be considered high without any sort of escalation from LFI to RFI.

Wrapping up, developing an internal complexity versus rating scale can be a useful way to prioritize vulnerabilities for remediation.

7.3.4 Ticketing and Internal SLA

The process of creating tickets and managing internal service level agreements that are defined within the enterprise is a unique, yet important, aspect of information security. During the ticket creation process, engineers managing the bug bounty program should use any integrations to ticket systems that the bug bounty platform may offer. Or in the unique instance that the enterprise is self-managing a program, engineers should define SLA management processes, which is discussed further in Chapter 9.

7.3.4.1 Creating Tickets

The vulnerability triage and validation process doesn't necessarily require program managers to make tickets internally. Managed services and triage employees cannot partake in such incentives. Normally, after the process of validating vulnerabilities and deeming them as reproducible and legitimate, first things first: *pay the researcher* if the vulnerability is valid, and due diligence has been performed to validate the issue. Obviously, ensure that the possibility of accidentally paying for a vulnerability that isn't valid doesn't exist before paying the researcher, as discussed previously.

Once the researcher is paid, connectors that integrate into most ticketing platforms will do the work of generating the report for the program internally. However, in some instances, the ticketing integration may not support the inclusion of the entire report. For example, as a bare minimum, a program will want to make sure of the following.

1. The ticket contains fully detailed steps.
   If triage or the security researcher writes steps that an application security engineer can understand, it doesn't necessarily mean that a software engineer will understand the same

steps. Translate any complex processes into easy-to-understand replication examples, something that someone who has limited technical experience may understand.

(Software engineers are highly technical, but understanding the exploitation process may require a different level of understanding.)

2. The ticket contains relevant files.

   In instances of exploitation where the security researcher uses an externally hosted file for a proof of concept, such as an HTML file, include this in the ticket. An engineer's time is valuable. Internal teams should not have to create any exploitation processes from scratch. If the researcher did not include the file, either ask for it or include the file that was used for validating the vulnerability.

3. The ticket contains proofs.

   Security researchers tend to include screenshots/videos of exploitation. If there's reason to believe that the exploit may be too complex to detail in several reproducible steps, be sure to include the material used to detail the exploitation process.

4. Additional information.

   Program managers should include any relevant information that wasn't parsed via the ticket integration functionality.

8

Vulnerability Disclosure Information

8.1 Understanding Public Disclosure

Program managers will typically have the ability to allow security researchers to disclose their findings after the issues are fixed. Allowing public disclosure of vulnerabilities isn't necessarily a program requirement, and program managers should be aware of any implications that may occur because of disclosure. Public disclosure, as it pertains to bug bounty platforms, is simply the act of allowing the report to populate via public feeds. It would be safe to assume that a report disclosed on the feed could possibly leave the platform in the form of writeups on the researcher's website, social media posts – or even journalists writing on the vulnerability.

8.1.1 Making the Decision

Ultimately, the decision to allow public disclosure depends on the objective of the program. The control of vulnerability remediation transparency (allow/deny) is up to the discretion of program managers. Still, it's important to understand that public programs have their own unique challenges in this process.

8.1.1.1 Private Programs

There are two ways that private programs can deal with vulnerability disclosure: one represents a standard built-in configuration use case, while the other is more of a decided-upon courtesy in support of the security researcher's efforts. Ultimately, it will also depend on the configuration allowances that a crowdsourcing platform determines. In most cases, private programs will have the ability to allow disclosure, although it's slightly different than what a program manager would expect from a public program.

1. Allowing Disclosure

The option to allow disclosure has to come from a place of understanding a security researcher's mentality, but also one of the potential enterprise impact. For example, consider the following.

A researcher works with the enterprise bug bounty program on a critical issue, one in which they could have been able to acquire hundreds of thousands of pieces of PII. Acting

Corporate Cybersecurity: Identifying Risks and the Bug Bounty Program, First Edition. John Jackson.
© 2021 John Wiley & Sons, Ltd. Published 2021 by John Wiley & Sons, Ltd.

in good faith, the security researcher stopped when they had access to the server, to avoid any accidental disclosure of PII.

If disclosure is allowed, most crowdsourcing platforms have policies in place where the only people that can view the disclosed (and patched) vulnerabilities are the other security researchers who have been invited to and are participating in the program. While most security researchers will have respect for the processes put in place for preventing disclosure of the vulnerability outside of the organization, that may not always be the case. A program manager shouldn't be presumptuous, but associated risk should be known.

The security researcher who found the vulnerability may not have any intention on the disclosure leaving the "feed" or "stream" in which it was shared with other researchers. If the enterprise is running a private program and participating in limited private disclosure, another researcher may take the report or the findings and leak the report to a journalist or online elsewhere. While the risk of such leakage occurring is exceedingly low, no one should ever assume that it could never happen. Ultimately, the damage that would be caused is one of reputation and not of exploitation as the vulnerability would be fixed. However, in reality, disclosure shouldn't be looked at as a means of reputation damage. When a program encourages disclosure, the community respects the enterprise far more.

2. Disclosure Restrictions

Program managers may decide to avoid disclosure altogether. In any case, the primary occasion in which an enterprise may not want limited disclosure may be due to fears of further exploitation or information leakage, outside of the control of the security researcher or program management.

Disclosure restrictions, at least from the perspective of program managers, are typically a result of immaturity in the bug bounty space. The exploitation of any disclosed report is improbable unless the report reveals more infrastructure or internal information on the program's private researcher feed. In any case, the information can typically be redacted prior to disclosing.

3. Ad Hoc Redactions

A lot of researchers participating in a private program will want disclosure, no matter what policy is currently in place. Security researchers may ask to redact information to be able to include it in their writeup. Instances where disclosure of this form is requested can occur if the enterprise's program only allows private-stream disclosure, or if the program allows no disclosure.

The Bottom Line

Security researchers value their research. If redaction can be done to support a researcher's disclosure, it would be a good incentive to do so in support of their participation. A program manager can write a clause in their program, or respond to researchers if asked, with the following:

"We will allow public disclosure in writeups. However, please give us the chance to review the writeup to ensure that no potential vectors for exploitation exist. We want you to share the research, but we would like to keep the company safe. We do not want to be overbearing, therefore it will be a light review. If you would prefer not to allow us to review the writeup, we understand and respect the value that you bring to our company. Disclose at will."

In most cases, a statement of support as defined above will be an adequate method of support for the security researcher's findings. Without falling subject to the fallacy of a slippery slope, completely preventing any form of public disclosure isn't useful methodology. Researchers who are avid writers that participate in the public-facing bug bounty community will end up disclosing, and this could result in accidentally disclosing internal information or infrastructure outside of the visibility or control of a program. Nonetheless, while it is an option to ask for redaction of specific aspects of the writeup, this should not be weaponized against a hacker. Redaction should only be done in a way that prevents further exploitation of the service. If a program manager does not feel comfortable with a researcher disclosing their research, they should aim to either improve security or refrain from operating a bug bounty program.

8.1.1.2 Public Programs

The subject of public programs represents a different challenge, the "anyone can do it" effect. In other words, an enterprise bug bounty program manager may find increased participation if participating researchers are allowed to disclose. Nearly all aspects of disclosure from private programs carry over to the configuration in public programs, with the exception of one additional feature that is reserved to public programs: full public disclosure.

1. Full Public Disclosure

Public programs have the ability to fully commit to the most permissive state of programs: full disclosure. Essentially, when an enterprise program is configured to have the disclosure feature in a public state, security researchers can request disclosure of their patched vulnerabilities, and that means the vulnerability will hit a highly visible state, one in which any person who accesses the crowdsourcing platform can completely see the report (with the desired redacted information).

One of the primary issues with fully public disclosure is the representation of a program's value and the possibility of increased participation (the anyone can do it effect). Basically, there are several scenarios in which full public disclosure can result in an excessive uptick of participation, primarily when a program discloses a vulnerability that resulted in a big reward or the program releases a chain of reports.

Payday mayday, or in summary, is the disclosure of a report in which a researcher has earned a significant amount of money, which could result in possible press. It's not unheard of to have a journalist write on the subject of a patched vulnerability, especially if it could have resulted in a significant exploitation or compromise of a user's data or a company's product. If a journalist picks up a vulnerability report and writes about it, a surge of researchers may rush to the program hoping for their shot at a big payday. Even though the instance of a vulnerability as critical as the disclosed one being found after the previous one was disclosed is unlikely, it's not impossible. Secondly, a burst of smaller vulnerabilities may be reported, or even if no greater-than-average amount of vulnerabilities get reported, there could be enterprise disruption as a result of a lot of security research activity being conducted. It's not a matter of fact that the vulnerability will be picked up by a journalist, but all scenarios should be considered.

Chain report disclosure may not result in press exposure, but comparatively, some similar effects seen in a high-payout scenario could possibly occur, particularly increased security researcher participation or disruptive levels of activity that the enterprise isn't ready to manage.

The Bottom Line

Program managers should allow public disclosure and realize that they need to be prepared to deal with a spike in reports, and have thoroughly hardened assets. The public disclosure process shouldn't be discouraged. However, if the enterprise is not comfortable with disclosure, realize that it's an uncomfortable event that program managers must get comfortable with. After all, even if the enterprise did not have a program, they face hackers disclosing vulnerabilities to the public. A program at least gives the chance to encourage positive rhetoric and rewards around reporting, giving program managers an edge. Allow researchers to disclose, or do not run a bug bounty program.

8.2 CVE Responsibility

8.2.1 What are CVEs?

CVEs stand for common vulnerabilities and exposures. The CVE program was developed in 1999 and is sponsored by the US Department of Homeland Security and the Cybersecurity and Infrastructure Security Agency. CVEs were meant to be used as a way of standardizing vulnerabilities and disclosures, linking many databases together in an attempt to make it easier for enterprises to manage and patch newly identified vulnerabilities.

8.2.2 Program Manager Responsibilities

A difficult aspect of bug bounty program management is to be on the lookout for CVEs, always. When the enterprise's product is involved, it could be more obvious that a CVE exists within the product if it requires patching a specific component that is used outside of the company. However, there are multiple instances that exist in which a CVE may be overlooked, and it's usually due to a lack of knowledge of the security research space. Both a security researcher and a program manager could end up overlooking the widespread impact of an identified vulnerability.

For these examples, we will use an enterprise that has a bug bounty program and specializes in providing Internet as a service, or in other words – an Internet Service Provider (ISP).

8.2.3 Hardware CVEs

An enterprise may offer a wide range of hardware, for instance in the case of the ISP their product could be a cable box or a router, and so on. If testing on routers were in scope, a researcher who finds a vulnerability within the router has likely successfully identified a CVE, but as stated, they may not know that the bug is a CVE which has a wider range of impact. Maintaining vigilance is important to ensure that the enterprise reduces impact and exploitability.

Scenario 1: SQL Injection on a Router

A researcher approaches the enterprise bug bounty program with a report that reads:

"Hello, I have found a vulnerability on the YNZX Router that is offered by your company. I noticed that I could perform a SQL Injection login bypass on the default gateway login page within my browser. For the username, I used admin and for the password I used: or '1' = '1

"Using the above payload allowed me to completely log in to the router without knowing the password at all. The payload will work in all scenarios in which the username 'admin' exists, or the SQL query can be modified to accommodate other usernames."

Evaluating Logic and Impact

The researcher's above payload essentially executes this SQL statement on the backend: SELECT * FROM users WHERE name = admin and password = or '1' = '1.

Or essentially, the username is presumed to be admin as that's typically default to most routers, and the password is bypassed because the statement password = "or'1' = 1" is a condition that is always true, so the password verification never happens. The researcher can now access the router configuration, which in any case is critical from the perspective of an unauthorized party. A threat actor, given the ability to log in to a Wi-Fi configuration for the entire LAN, can do a lot of damage to the network.

First, understanding that the exploitation of the router on LAN hardly reduces impact. Businesses commonly maintain guest networks for their clients or customers. Therefore, a threat actor can undoubtedly pivot into the network. In some cases, the exploitation case could be simpler than described, where a business doesn't create segmentation between guest Wi-Fi and the enterprise Wi-Fi.

The enterprise operating the bug bounty program now has a unique situation in their hands. After testing on their own local equipment, it was determined that it could be replicated. In a situation as described, a zero-day vulnerability (never before seen) exists and the enterprise knows that a patch will have to be published. Of course, the ISP has the ability to ignore any possibility of reporting a CVE. However, the ability to control the flow of information and how it's presented is a necessity for business reputation. Adequate public disclosure attributes a far better reputation to a company than a researcher having to deal with the process themselves or journalists getting involved in processes, on some occasions with limited experience of the exploitation that has occurred.

When an enterprise runs into a situation as such, they should report the CVE on behalf of the researcher. Typically, internal company oversight will allow better visibility into the product patching and management processes, which will produce a much more valuable report. Exceedingly mature companies will have their own CNAs (CVE numbering authorities) that can assign CVE numbers on behalf of the researcher and announce the vulnerabilities to the public.

In most instances, CNAs aren't a resource that the majority of program managers will be able to utilize. Instead, follow the guidelines outlined in Section 8.3.2.

8.2.4 Software and Product CVEs

The same ISP may have a premium video streaming service that's served via an application that users may purchase as an addition to their monthly bill. The application is served via a connection that is made externally over the Internet, and isn't a web-based asset. In fact, it's downloaded as an executable (.exe) file, with a separate version for MAC (.dmg). Additionally, the application allows users to create accounts and share their video lists with other users, and view recent activity on their profile page.

Scenario 2: Stored XSS Vulnerability

The bug bounty program run by the enterprise receives a report from a researcher:

"I have identified a vulnerability in which I can produce a stored cross-site scripting (XSS) vulnerability. First, I went to the 'username' field of the application's profile page, and clicked on 'edit.' Next, I entered the payload < script > alert(1) </script > and clicked on the 'save' button. The application allowed me to save the payload as my username, and it immediately triggered a XSS vulnerability. In addition, I had my brother view my account using his application from a different computer and upon viewing my account, an alert of "1' popped up."

Evaluating logic and impact
Simply put, the lack of sanitization allowed this alert to be stored and served to users who view the researcher's profile page. The alert popping up when viewed by other users is problematic because it could allow a threat actor to perform social engineering attacks, potentially stealing other users' information or even taking over their accounts. The impact could be substantial because some information can be gathered without a user's interaction at all. Nonetheless, in normal circumstances a regular patch to the application will fix the issue.

The application was unfortunately produced in such a way that updates cannot be forced upon a user. Instead, a user will be urged to update the application and can continue to ignore the update for as long as they possibly desire. It's clear to the organization that they will need to disclose the vulnerability to the public to reduce impact or company reputation damage. The process of reporting the vulnerability will be similar to the reporting method stated in the previous scenario.

8.2.5 Third-party CVEs

In the previous two scenarios, the requirement for public vulnerability disclosure and patching was presented directly to the organizations, but what happens in the circumstance that it's not clear? In the example scenario with the ISP, one could now imagine that their web application is using a wide array of third-party software integrations and code. For this specific scenario, let's create two fictional company names – Ryudar the ISP and AppAncors, a vendor they use for link anchors and redirects.

Scenario 3: Remote code execution on partner software

In this scenario, a researcher submits a vulnerability through the program that reads:

"Hi team, I have identified another vulnerability. This time, I noticed that I was able to get remote code execution on your website. First, I was clicking on some of the links on the website for some of your submenus and when I clicked on one and intercepted the request, I noticed this:

https://rudar.appsancors.com/example.php?page=/home

The page = parameter in conjunction with PHP sparked my interest. Knowing that I could possibly get LFI (local file inclusion) or RFI (remote file inclusion), I began testing. First, I edited the/home section of the page = parameter to php://input and added the '&' character with cmd = ls:

https://rudar.appsancors.com/example.php?page=php://input&cmd=ls

In the body of the post request, I put the following code:

<?php echo shell_exec($_GET('cmd'));?>

"As a result, I was able to see all of the files in the root file directory of the HTTP server. Using various reverse shell one-liners, I was able to get a reverse shell on the server – allowing full remote code execution."

Evaluating logic and impact

Objectively analyzing the data, it seems sound. The researcher was successfully able to demonstrate remote code execution, and minimal effort resulted in a reverse shell situation, which could have been deadly to the organization. Allowing users to manipulate parameters without the server checking for the authenticity and anti-tampering logic makes this bug a major vulnerability – so what's the issue? Review the site URL:

ryudar.appsancors.com

The issue quickly becomes clear. The domain name is "appsancors" and the subdomain is "ryudar" – simply put, the security researcher accidentally believed that the indication of ryudar indicated that the asset was in scope. It was an honest mistake, and can happen to the best researchers. In this instance AppsAncors manages services for Ryudar and they are likely hosting subdomains for multiple organizations. With this being the case, simply using a different subdomain for another organization that uses the services results in the exact same vulnerability.

The triage team may or may not notice that it's out of scope and bring attention to the vulnerability. Nonetheless, the program manager will determine that it's out of scope, as a result of a flaw in the vendor's product if triaged correctly. The tricky part is determining how to manage the resolution going forward, but there are several methods that can be used.

8.3 Submission Options

Whether it's the responsibility of a program manager to submit the vulnerability or not completely depends on the vulnerability submitted and the coordination that takes place. There are several options for reporting the vulnerability, and it's subject to change. Program managers should understand the various scenarios that can occur during the reporting process and realize that CVE management is dynamic. As always, the best interests of both the enterprise bug bounty program and the researcher should be kept in mind at all times.

8.3.1 In-house Submissions

The standard in-house submissions are usually the easiest because they defer to internal processes that have already been established (i.e. CNA). If a program manager is confused about whether their enterprise is a CNA, they should refer to the comprehensive list of CNAs (https://cve.mitre.org/cve/request_id.html#cna_participants), and keep in mind that the probability of an enterprise having a CNA without the security team knowing about it is fairly unlikely. If the enterprise does indeed have a CNA, best practice would be to patch the vulnerability, and submit the CVE via the reporting system that the CNA has access to (https://cve.mitre.org/cve/cna/Requesting_Blocks_of_CVE_IDs-for_CNAs_only.pdf) if the enterprise running a program has a large enough use case to become a CNA, please use the following form:

(https://cve.mitre.org/cve/cna.html#become_a_cna)

8.3.2 Program Managed Submissions and Hands-off Submissions

An enterprise should allow the researcher the opportunity to submit the CVE themselves if they so wish. However, ask the researcher if they would allow the program to disclose on their behalf. Realistically speaking, the program reserves the right to do so because of the bug bounty program nondisclosure agreements, but they should not be depended on exclusively.

8.3.2.1 Program Managed Submissions

If a vulnerable component is identified that may affect more than just one user and requires a CVE disclosure, follow a set of submission steps.

Steps to Submit

1. First, tell the researcher that the vulnerability has been identified as a CVE (if this wasn't in the program).
2. Tell the researcher that you would prefer that the enterprise goes through the submission process, but ask if the researcher is okay with that.
3. If the researcher does not establish a deadline, offer 90 days for the patching process before submitting. If the vulnerability will likely be much sooner, be sure to express that. It's probable that the researcher will disclose far sooner than the full 90-day period, especially if the issue is critical.

4. The program manager should first coordinate with the appropriate internal team to ask them to fix the issue. Next, the program should go to MITRE's website and submit the official CVE ID request form.
5. When MITRE processes the request, a CVE ID will be assigned and they will wait for references, or in other words, a proof of concept or advisory from the affected party, confirming a fix.
6. Program managers can submit the references via replying to the CVE assignment email, and then MITRE will publicly publish the CVE. If timing permits and the researcher has taken responsible measures, the actual bug bounty report can be disclosed and used as the primary reference.

Note: social media handles or temporary posts on social media are insufficient references. In order to protect the enterprise, at a minimum, submit one reference from the enterprise such as a bug bounty report, patch notice, or GitHub pull request, and so on.

8.3.2.2 Hands-off Submissions

If after collaboration, the program and researcher agree to a self-submission approach, the security researcher is agreeing to manage interactions. There are several instances in which this would occur. For example, a vulnerability identified on a third party would constitute a hands-off approach, and this would likely be non-negotiable on behalf of the researcher as it's not the responsibility of the enterprise to disclose vulnerabilities for products they don't own. Program managers should let the researcher know that they will have to contact the affected party. Additionally, there's the possibility of a researcher wanting to disclose the CVE to MITRE themselves. In this instance, discuss how it can be done safely, and kindly ask the researcher to provide the proposed submission to MITRE. Validating the submission will adequately enable the enterprise bug bounty program to ensure that the security researcher is effectively describing and capturing the vulnerability, affected version, or severity levels.

Note: do *not* attempt to provoke the security researcher or threaten legal action. Attempt to understand the case for disclosure, and so on. Mitigating negative interactions is an essential part of provoking positive research, as markets where researchers can sell CVEs exist. The researcher chose to adequately report an issue that may have been worth a lot of money otherwise.

Submission Example

The following is an example submission that may be sent to MITRE, with the intent of showing program managers what a CVE form will look like when done correctly.

MITRE CVE Form

Other vulnerability type
SQL Injection
Vendor of the product(s)
Fake Vendor

Affected product(s)/code base
Line 1: Fake Vendor Desktop Client, Windows & macOS
Line 2: Versions ⩽ 3.26
Has vendor confirmed or acknowledged the vulnerability?
No
Other impact
Inefficient Special Character Sanitization
Affected component(s)
/api/?url = web application parameter
Attack vector(s)
Remote
Suggested description of the vulnerability for use in the CVE
SQL Injection affects the/api/?url = parameter via API calls that are made between the Fake Vendor Desktop Client versions ⩽ 3.26 for both Windows & macOS. An attack can pass UNION SQL injection payloads, resulting in the exposure of sensitive information.
Discoverer(s)/Credits
Alice Bobby & Bobby Alice
Reference(s)
Provided upon patch, or 30–90 days thereafter.
Additional information
N/A

Once the form is submitted, typically the organization will patch and then provide a patch notice or writeup (aka references) to MITRE and then MITRE will officially release the CVE to the public.

Part 5

Internal and External Communication

9

Development and Application Security Collaboration

9.1 Key Role Differences

The application security and development roles are vastly different in both workflow and responsibility. Obviously, depending on the enterprise, the roles can vary dramatically and the enterprise program may be composed of information security practitioners, and not necessarily application security engineers acting as bug bounty program managers.

9.1.1 Application Security Engineer

During the program process, application security engineers are responsible for the consistent evaluation of security programs as it pertains to the enterprises applications such as websites, mobile apps, and third-party reviews, especially if partners use any of the applications in a privileged manner. Typically, an application security engineer will be responsible for the security during the development of the applications and all of the processes involved.

9.1.2 Development

Primarily, software engineers will acquire the brunt of the workload involved with remediating vulnerabilities that have been established. However, that's not always the case. Depending on the identified issue, application security engineers will find that they may have to collaborate with other teams, such as cloud security or infrastructure teams, to resolve identified vulnerabilities. The resolution of vulnerabilities does not solely fall into the bracket of software engineering.

Note: even though application security engineers are responsible for evaluating and remediating security issues, the various application creators and maintainers must exercise good secure coding practices.

Corporate Cybersecurity: Identifying Risks and the Bug Bounty Program, First Edition. John Jackson.
© 2021 John Wiley & Sons, Ltd. Published 2021 by John Wiley & Sons, Ltd.

9.2   Facing a Ticking Clock

It shouldn't come at a surprise that the responsible program managers will have quite a few hurdles to face when dealing with vulnerability remediation. Obviously, the expectation to resolve the identified vulnerabilities comes from both the security researcher and enterprise program perspective. For example, if multiple identified vulnerabilities are validated, ensuring that criticality is prioritized is an absolute necessity, and will help in the ticking clock also known as a service level agreement (SLA). Researchers are eager to resolve issues, and program managers will likely be facing anxious researchers constantly asking for updates. While a swift resolution isn't guaranteed in all scenarios, the important part is ensuring that both researchers and management understand the level of effort required.

Imagine a scenario in which a vulnerability was identified that has a recommended remediation timeline of two full weeks. Program managers should be proactive about the resolution and communicate any blockers to anyone involved. If a researcher expects updates throughout the period and receives zero updates, they will get discouraged. They will become even more discouraged if the expected service level agreement time isn't met. Instead of apologies post-failed criteria, it doesn't hurt to update the researcher before the missed deadline, explaining various blockers in the resolution process. The program manager responsible for facilitating communication doesn't necessarily have to divulge too much information about the blockers, but an update is usually appreciated.

In conjunction with keeping researchers updated, program managers must prioritize blockers to leadership. If leadership has to consistently ask for updates on vulnerabilities, it can impact the workflow and create an unnecessary sense of urgency for the teams responsible for patching the identified vulnerability. If leadership has to intervene during the remediation process too often, software engineers or other responsible development parties may feel as if vulnerabilities are being blown out of proportion when collaborating in the future.

9.3   Meaningful Vulnerability Reporting

Often, engineers make the mistake of relaying reported vulnerabilities to software engineers in an overly technical way. Even though software engineers are highly technical individuals, exploitation is a different art and in some instances the vulnerability may be overlooked or misunderstood if reported incorrectly. As anything, program managers should learn how the different teams within the organization operate and adjust according. How does one define "overly technical"? First and foremost, it's unlikely that a software engineer would ever admit to a report being outside of their range of understanding. There's no specific threshold for a report being too technical. Therefore, program managers should strive to relay vulnerabilities in a way that everyone can understand. There's no such thing as a report being "too easy to understand."

Compare two excerpts from the same report, translated with two separate summaries, and notice differences in the effectiveness of the following relayed report.

Report 1

Summary: insufficient RegEx in private-ip npm package v1.0.5 and below insufficiently filters reserved IP ranges resulting in indeterminate server-side request forgery (SSRF). An attacker can perform a large range of requests to ARIN (American Registry for Internet Numbers) reserved IP ranges, resulting in an indeterminable number of critical attack vectors, allowing remote attackers to request server-side resources or potentially execute arbitrary code through various SSRF techniques.

Report 2

Summary: security researcher was able to abuse the private-ip npm package to bypass IP range restrictions, resulting in a SSRF vulnerability. It's not clear how many payloads can be used to bypass the SSRF restrictions. However, the lack of restriction resulted in the researcher being able to interact with internal resources, resulting in a critical vulnerability.

Even though both of the summaries are true, Report 2's summary is friendlier for presentation to a software engineer or other development team. Paired with easy-to-understand steps, Report 2 will surpass the presentation of Report 1. Communicating the information in a concise way that gets to the root of the vulnerability is essential to prevent mishaps or delays in any of the resolution processes. The replication steps should be written about in a similar sense. When attempting to summarize the replication steps, refrain from using highly technical terms if there's an easier way of explaining things. Although there isn't a set way to accomplish this, two ways a program manager can alleviate the stress of a software engineer or other responsible party from feeling bogged down are minimizing the number of steps it will take to replicate the vulnerability or, if all the steps are necessary, avoiding acronyms and providing the "why" a bug is a particular issue.

For example, a software engineer may be familiar with the term "XSS" but when a program manager first starts, they should expand upon the abbreviation, (cross-site scripting). In addition, an engineer may not know what cross-site scripting is. Typically, a quick blurb, such as: "Cross-site scripting (aka XSS) is a method in which an attack can steal information from a user via social engineering," is a good way to explain quick risk. Refer to the OWASP Top Ten guide to understand a little more about application vulnerabilities (https://owasp.org/www-project-top-ten/).

9.4 Communicating Expectations

One of the ways program managers risk hurting the potential for success in an enterprise bug bounty program is with unrealistic expectations or being too lax in management processes. Program managers should maintain a balanced approach to achieve the best possible outcome, adjusting based on the severity of the vulnerability. It's typically unwise to set high expectations on a low severity vulnerability, as it can potentially damage the relationship between the program manager and responsible remediating party. Similarly, setting low expectations can cause just as much harm to the program's reputation, especially if engineers don't believe they are being held accountable to fix the issues. Whatever timelines are agreed upon, both software development managers and security managers should have full oversight of the remediation process to prevent any unnecessary disagreements.

In addition, encourage software engineers to add comments to any vulnerability tickets to update the application security team of progress. While not every software engineer has a workflow that includes consistent communication via comments, the idea in mind is to maintain an open dialogue in the resolution process. No single software engineer is alike and program managers should strive to make determinations of all of the effective communication processes and adjust accordingly.

9.5 Pushback, Escalations, and Exceptions

The responsibility of professional accountability falls on the program manager. Whether discussing timelines provided for software engineers or executive management, the one key point of understanding is to know that, no matter what, the program managers will be held responsible for the remediation of any vulnerabilities. Since program managers are held accountable, understanding when to escalate on responsible parties is a necessary truth, but it doesn't have to be a toxic interaction. For example, imagine that a software engineer was given two full weeks to remediate a SSRF vulnerability. During the process, the program manager communicates expectations and the software engineer immediately says, "I'm not going to have enough time to fix this. This incentive needs to wait until the end of the month." Realistically, since the vulnerability is rated as a high severity with the potential of easily turning into a critical, the remediation process cannot afford to wait too long. While it may seem embarrassing to talk about how to talk, a bug bounty program will fail if program managers don't have the power to push back. The most effective way to ensure the bug bounty program is taken seriously is to define steps and methodologies internally and externally, that everyone can refer to.

9.5.1 Internal steps

- Develop a team board or way to track resolution processes. It can be as simple as a list of tickets and due dates, or as extensive as full story tracking, such as with the capabilities that agile methodologies bring to the table.
- Create a playbook as a means of explaining processes. Executive leadership may not be heavily involved in the application security workflows. A playbook can be an excellent way to present key pieces of information, such as company policy on vulnerability resolution expectations, managing issues or exceptions, and so on. In addition, more information can always be worked into the runbook to elaborate on any defined workflows to junior engineers who may not have had to deal with security issues.
- Reiterate the processes to responsible impacted teams, even if it's believed that the team may know what they are doing. For example, a simple: "Hello, we identified a vulnerability with X component on X application. The expectation is to get this resolved within (X weeks or months) as the criticality of the vulnerability is (low/medium/high/

critical) and might result in negative possibilities if exploited by a threat actor." Program managers will find far greater success if thorough yet useful expectations and risk analyses are conducted and relayed in a meaningful way.

9.5.2 External steps

- Establish SLA times within the bug bounty program description to hold internal teams accountable for resolution, ideally something that meets or is close to internally defined times.
- Exclude security researchers from internal communication processes. It's important to prevent any advanced oversight of the relationship between the program manager and different development aspects of security. The program manager's main priority is to validate, resolve, and pay researchers for vulnerabilities. Therefore, it's pertinent to prevent speculation or demotivation.

9.5.2 Escalations

To be completely transparent, it may be difficult or even feel discouraging to have to deal with engineers who are not apt to maintain a good vulnerability resolution track record. As an information security professional, managing relationships with nonsecurity personnel will always be difficult. Whether the issue at large is miscommunication, demotivation, or disrespect, speculation can be harmful and permanently damage relationships with colleagues who will inevitably have to assist if any vulnerabilities are identified in their space. Evaluate the following scenarios of communications between a senior application security engineer and a software engineer and read the various analyses, noting which situations may need escalation depending on the program manager's leadership style, defined resolution times, and preferences.

1. *Scenario: miscommunication* Shanice talks to Ricardo about an XSS vulnerability that has been identified. She notices that the ticket hasn't been updated with any progress and the deadline indicates that the ticket is two days overdue. In addition, a week prior to the deadline Shanice informed her manager that she believed Ricardo might miss the deadline, and her manager is informed that she will be looped in on Shanice's follow-up emails. She has talked to Ricardo and his manager on multiple occasions about the deadline via email, in which Ricardo's manager responded with a claim that it would be finished in time.

   Analysis: Shanice maintained the right principles throughout the process but overall there's still a level of disconnect between the application security team and the engineering team. Shanice has followed up with the team on multiple occasions to check on the progress of the work, and the responsible team has reassured her that it would be taken care of. Even though assurance was provided, the responsible team did not contact Shanice about the possibility of missing the deadline, even with her manager involved in the interaction. In this particular scenario, Shanice should make a recommendation to her manager that escalation to the next level of leadership should occur. Typically, this would have been best addressed several days prior to the missed deadline. However, responsibility isn't always claimed and program managers must maintain some level of responsibility for failures of miscommunication as well.

2. *Scenario: Demotivation* Shanice receives a message from James stating that he's having a lot of issues resolving the sensitive information disclosure vulnerability that was assigned to him. James also seems to be stressed out about the 30-day timeline resolution requirement, stating that it's difficult to prioritize and resolve this. Shanice doesn't specifically know how to resolve the vulnerability, but she knows that another software engineer, Rachel, has dealt with this issue. Shanice offers to have a call and bring Rachel on to advise. Reluctantly, James accepts the meeting and allows Rachel to talk him through the resolution process. Shanice interjections about timelines and expectations where needed.

   Analysis: Shanice made the right call. Rather than scorn the engineer for not knowing how to fix the vulnerability, she decided to kindly reach out to another engineer and coordinate a meeting with James. In this specific scenario, Shanice did not need to escalate, because there was plenty of time remaining for the resolution process and a lack of any major issues.

3. *Scenario: Disrespect* On a Friday, a security researcher identifies a critical remote code execution vulnerability. Shanice gathers all of the information, and immediately reports it to her manager, who also informs the chief information security officer. The affected team, the API development team, only has two employees (a manager and Jaycee, the principal software engineer). Shanice reaches out to Jaycee about the vulnerability and is ignored for several hours. After finally touching base with the engineer, Jaycee responds and states she doesn't believe the vulnerability really matters, and that she has higher priorities. Shanice explains why it matters, in a professional manner, and Jaycee escalates – stating that she has better things to do than deal with this and she can wait until Monday morning. Quickly, Shanice tries to refute this, but Jaycee stops responding. Jaycee's manager catches wind of the situation and tries to work it out with Shanice, but ultimately agrees that the team doesn't believe it matters and that the team's workflow is already heavy.

   Analysis: in this situation, Shanice approached the scenario correctly from a professional perspective, but could use a bit of guidance on proper escalation procedures. Explaining the criticality and why a vulnerability matters to software engineers is an essential skill that all program managers must acquire. However, this scenario seems particularly heated, at least from Shanice's perspective. When a scenario becomes negative enough that a software engineer believes they can say no and ignore the security team, a program manager should immediately escalate to leadership. When a vulnerability is critical enough, program managers should put reservations of escalation aside and think about the security of the enterprise. Failure to remediate quickly could be enough for an organization to fail to protect user data, infrastructure or other key components of the organization.

9.5.3 Summary

The scenarios described in the examples are not the only issues that can happen in the bug bounty resolution lifecycle. The key takeaway is understanding that program managers must appropriately use critical thinking to adequately think on their feet and resolve issues in a logical manner. It's not appropriate to unnecessarily escalate issues that can be resolved or ignore issues that should clearly be escalated. Maintaining a kind but fair approach is the best way a program manager can operate the bug bounty program successfully, throughout the entire lifecycle.

9.6 Continuous Accountability

Program managers have an obligation to follow up in the vulnerability remediation process. Assigning vulnerability tickets to affected teams with no due date, or not actually following up with the teams for remediation, is a simple way to burn money and tank a bug bounty program. Security researchers will want their issues to be resolved, but this cannot happen when teams are not being held accountable. Although a close relative of the category of escalation, continuous accountability is the full responsibility of the program manager.

9.6.1 Tracking

Proper accountability is more or less a matter of ensuring that all of the vulnerabilities that have been communicated are tracked from start to finish. It's highly recommended to use the ticketing processes described in Chapter 7. Technically, a program manager can maintain vulnerabilities however they want, but ticketing systems such as Jira are the preferred methodologies to maintain full oversight of any blockers in the vulnerability resolution process.

9.6.2 Missed Deadlines

In reality, it would be extremely unfair to assume that a bug bounty program will maintain the SLA in every scenario. Even the best program managers can possibly miss a deadline, and the same can be said about the top software engineers. Life happens, and the vital takeaway piece of information is to remember to stay calm in the instance of a missed deadline. A few key steps will prevent a missed deadline from turning into a disaster:

1. First and foremost, notify leadership. Bug bounty programs cannot be effective if transparency isn't maintained. However, don't notify leadership without a plan, and there's no need to escalate if there's a fairly good reason for why the deadline was missed. For example, if a software engineer did not meet the deadline by a day because of something else that went wrong in the production environment, generally speaking a program manager would notify leadership of the deadline. However, if, for instance, the program manager forgot about a vulnerability and then it was two months overdue, transparency with leadership is essential. Being honest is of paramount importance.
2. Communicate about the issue. Maintain communication with the appropriate team to resolve the issue. Inform them that it's overdue and explain the importance of fixing the vulnerability.
3. Notify the researcher. Obviously, letting the researcher know that the resolution is in progress is important. However, this is not nearly as important as actually fixing the issue or notifying leadership of any blockers in the resolution process.

10

Hacker and Program Interaction Essentials

10.1 Understanding the Hacker

A program manager should never automatically assume that the hacker holds "x" intention. Security research is delicate, but the common misconception is that hackers are motivated by money. Many program managers don't understand the value of security research until they've been managing a bug bounty program for a while. Understanding why a hacker participates isn't always as simple as it seems.

10.1.1 Money, Ethics, or Both?

Hackers' motivations vary. Some hackers are from countries where the value of the US dollar scales exceedingly well with their local currency. Therefore, even smaller payouts can work wonders. Researchers that are motivated to work for money aren't necessarily unethical, and shouldn't be viewed as such – after all, bug bounty hunting is a day job for many across the world. Bug bounty program managers should consider the possibility that the security researcher reporting the vulnerability could rely on it as their primary source of income, and treat all researchers as full-time professionals. The suggestion to consider full-time bounty hunters' need for money isn't affirmation to pay for invalid bugs, simply something to remember when realizing the amount of power that program managers amass. There's nothing wrong with a security researcher being financially motivated. A program manager should not be fearful of a researcher who approaches and immediately asks about financial reward. The researcher could mean well, and that most often appears to be the case. Always be wary of exploitation attempts, but presumptions of a researcher's bad intentions can be detrimental. Always gather information first.

Believe it or not, there are security researchers out there that could care less about money. Several components exist that are worrisome in this regard. For one, it's undeniable that researchers that could care less about money are fairly easygoing people. It takes a lot of spirit and commitment to hacking in order to be transparent and honest enough to disclose a vulnerability to a program, knowing right well that a payment for research may not be provided (for an out-of-scope or disqualifying vulnerability.) Easygoing researchers may lull some project managers into a belief that they don't need to be too forthcoming with payments, and this can jeopardize the future of vulnerability research. Imagine that

Corporate Cybersecurity: Identifying Risks and the Bug Bounty Program, First Edition. John Jackson.
© 2021 John Wiley & Sons, Ltd. Published 2021 by John Wiley & Sons, Ltd.

program managers become used to a handful of researchers who are easygoing and decide to report vulnerabilities, even if they are out of scope, and don't express any interest in payment. Researchers can inadvertently lead to programs not expanding the scope or program managers opting out of bug bounty programs to offer proprietary programs where no rewards are offered. One could argue that it's a fallacious line of thinking, possibly even a slippery slope. However, the point here is to ensure that security researchers receive their due. If a researcher reports a vulnerability that's in scope but says, "You don't have to pay me," it is still always best to respond with "Are you sure? We would really like to pay you for your efforts." Giving the researcher the opportunity to at least be rewarded for their work can help avoid corruption or unrealistic expectations creeping into a program based on past experiences with easygoing researchers.

The in-between are researchers who represent both a desire for money and a willingness to ignore the monetary aspect if push comes to shove. The majority of researchers tend to fall into this category of hacking. Researchers that don't hack for the money, or for the pure ethics of the craft, are known as in-between researchers. Money doesn't usually come into the argument; however, the in-between researchers don't necessarily say no to adequate payment.

However, it's not unusual to see this category of researchers first ask for money and disclose anyway if there isn't a financial benefit.

Note: the following case studies are real, but the company names have been redacted to provide anonymity to the organizations.

Case Study 1 – Money

A researcher once reached out to a "security@anonymouscompany.com" contact with the following email:

"Your company is extremely vulnerable to a certain attack that I have identified. If you're interested in knowing what the vulnerability is, you will have to promise to pay me money. I don't work for free. You may be interested in this, as it's a critical matter."

The responding company had a bug bounty program and offered to onboard the researcher, suggesting that the vulnerability be reported through the program. The researcher responded that they would only report the vulnerability if it were on an asset that was in scope, and the company agreed. After onboarding the researcher, they reported the vulnerability quickly (because it was in scope) and the program promptly paid the researcher for their work. The company did make note of the severity of the vulnerability, which was not nearly as severe as the researcher had claimed originally.

Case Study 2 – Ethics

Company X operated a bug bounty program. On a particular Tuesday morning, they received a report from a researcher claiming to have remote code execution on one of the servers for a subdomain. Although it was out of scope, the researcher reported it and in the report said, "I'm seriously not in this for the money" and self-closed the report before the triage team could respond to the vulnerability. Company X validated that the server hosting the subdomain in question was indeed vulnerable to the remote code execution vulnerability identified by the researcher.

Case Study 3 – Hybrid

Via social media, the social media management team for Company X was made aware of a vulnerability a researcher had identified. The social media team bridged the communication between the researcher and the security team for the company. Before the vulnerability disclosure process, the researcher said, "Does Company X have a bug bounty program? I am hoping to be rewarded for my vulnerability findings; however, I understand if no such program is available."

Company X responded to the researcher that they did not have a bug bounty program. The researcher affirmed that it was OK, and responsibly disclosed all of their vulnerability findings to the company, expecting nothing in return.

10.1.2 Case Study Analysis

When reviewing all of the case studies, identifying major defining differences between all of the researchers is a simple task. The ethical and monetary approaches can have negative consequences for the future of researchers, and operating a fair program will ensure that researchers receive their due diligence. For example, in Case Study 1, the researcher was clearly interested in money from the get-go. An inexperienced program manager might be very wary of a researcher immediately discussing payment and refusing to disclose otherwise. However, it's necessary to understand that taking all reports seriously is the responsibility of a program manager, and even if the researcher sounds threatening, enterprises have an obligation to respond to the researcher to a certain extent. Every situation should be managed diligently, and understanding the perspective of a researcher is important to understanding their intention for hacking and participating in programs.

10.2 Invalidating False Positives

One of the most difficult aspects of managing bug bounty programs is the process of invalidating false positives. Most individuals don't want the responsibility of having to tell a security researcher that the identified issue isn't actually a problem at all. Unfortunately, this is the burden program managers have a responsibility to bear. Managing a false positive can feel embarrassing at first, but there are ways to manage the occurrence professionally.

10.2.1 Intake Process and Breaking the News

As a program manager, the false positive rate should be relatively low if the enterprise has a bug bounty platform. The triage team for the platform will maintain the responsibility of validating to ensure that it's a true positive, but in some instances false positives will accidentally get triaged. First and foremost, a program manager should never create a ticket and assign it to an engineering team without first validating that the vulnerability is legitimate. Avoiding the situation of going through the entire triage process will ensure that program managers and affected teams don't bear the burden of having more steps than necessary if a vulnerability is invalid. Once the vulnerability is deemed invalid, program managers should calmly inform the security researcher that a mistake was made, without pointing their finger at the triage team. The following is a good example of a fictional scenario, and the appropriate way to manage the situation and address the security researcher:

Nick is the program manager for Company X. The bug bounty program that he manages receives a report on a Friday evening about a cross-site request forgery (CSRF) vulnerability, resulting in the theft of sensitive data from a user. During the weekend, the triage team evaluates the vulnerability and notes that it's a true positive. The triage team cleans up the report, produces a subreport with easy-to-follow vulnerability replication steps, and assigns the ticket to Nick's team for further review. Nick doesn't have a lot of experience with hacking, but is excellent in the code review process. After reviewing the researcher's proof of concept, Nick is having issues understanding how this is a vulnerability. Typically, a standard CSRF vulnerability proof of concept would result in the security researcher being able to prove that sensitive data can be stolen. When a domain's access control allow origin is too permissive and the access-control-allow-credentials is set to "true" it can result in someone being able to steal credentials.

The issue that Nick is facing appears to be one in which sensitive information that is being returned is nonexistent. When Nick executes the researcher's proof of concept script, he notices that the only information being returned to the page is source code for the page and a few other minor details, but nothing deemed a security risk. To ensure that he isn't overlooking something important, Nick decides to host his own separate proof of concept and, again, notes that no sensitive data is being returned. Nick's overall verdict is that the research is indeed able to exploit the overly permissive cross-origin resource sharing (CORS) policy. However, the exploitation occurs on a page that has no sensitive data at all and does not impact the confidentiality, integrity, or availability of any user or enterprise data. Additionally, the occurrence of this false positive has been identified a long time prior to the bug bounty program inviting hackers. In fact, Nick ensured that in the out-of-scope section there was a specific clause that stated exploitation on pages that had no provable impact was to be considered out of scope. Nick did not open a ticket, and began to prepare communications with the security researcher.

Now that it has been established that a false positive exists, Nick has to break the news to the security researcher.

NICK: After further validation, we've noted that the CSRF vulnerability you are reporting is actually a false positive. We are sorry for the mix-up, and hope you continue to participate in our program.

RESEARCHER: I don't understand. The program said this was a verified vulnerability and I was even able to pull sensitive information from the page.

NICK: I understand and I apologize. However, we had noted that there isn't any sensitive information actually being displayed in this vulnerability. Even when logged into a user account and clicking on the CSRF that is externally hosted, no sensitive information, tokens, or anything that can be used for nefarious purposes was able to be retrieved.

RESEARCHER: I think the information is sensitive and that I should be compensated for the vulnerability. This is clearly a CSRF vulnerability.

NICK: Yes, this is a CSRF vulnerability but in our program out-of-scope section we highlight the following:

"Any CSRF vulnerabilities that are not on the login page or able to disclose sensitive information."

In addition, this isn't sensitive data. The information being returned by your CSRF script is the source code of the page, which is publicly visible to all. Please go to the domain and inspect the code and attempt to find it. You will note that the CSRF vulnerability proof of concept that you provided pulled code from there. We will be happy to reconsider if you can demonstrate a valid proof of concept that is within the scope of our program.

RESEARCHER: OK, I took a look and this appears to be true. I'm sorry for reporting this.

NICK: Don't be sorry! We appreciate your participation, thank you.

While this was a difficult conversation for Nick to have, it's important to ensure that false positives are deemed as such. Paying for one could be the difference between negative interactions in the future, although program managers shouldn't take it to heart in the event of an honest mistake. It may seem unlikely that both a triager and program manager fail and pay for a nonissue, but nothing is impossible. Keeping false positives in mind and being willing to tell a security researcher "no" is a nonnegotiable aspect of bug bounty program management.

10.2.2 Dealing with a Toxic Hacker

The time will eventually come when a program manager has to deal with a security researcher who has now become toxic or exceedingly difficult to deal with. In some cases, the program manager may not have to deal with a negative security researcher immediately. The point they decide to cause issues can vary, such as before the ticket is addressed, during the vulnerability remediation process, or after. Each situation must be handled delicately as there's a possibility it can end up completely working against the enterprise, or the researcher, and neither is ideal. How is a toxic interaction defined? Unfortunately, it's difficult to define what "toxic" is, but generally it's an exceedingly negative interaction in which the program manager has no choice but to implement drastic measures to resolve the behavior.

Toxic scenario examples

- A researcher believes that their vulnerability is more serious than the enterprise or triage team does, resulting in arguments.
- A nonenterprise asset vulnerability is reported, such as a third-party vendor, and the researcher wants to be paid.
- The researcher has completely violated the scope of the program and wants to be paid for their research.

10.3   Managed Program Considerations

As discussed in Chapter 3 (Section 3.7), managed programs are an excellent way to offset some of the inevitable grief that will be experienced from program management. If a security researcher reports a vulnerability and it's not actually an issue, a triager can quickly resolve the issue. In the instance a security researcher decides to become toxic, it's even easier for a bug bounty program manager to deal with because they now have the ability to moderate and participate at will and are not quite emotionally attached to the situation. Bug bounty platform solutions will typically have the means to resolve toxic interactions fairly quickly. Here are some general considerations when observing interactions between the bug bounty platform triage team and the security researcher:

1. Without having to ask, a program manager should be able to determine what the dispute is about via reading through the various communications.
2. If the dispute is about the legitimacy of a vulnerability, validate the triager's response. For example, a triager may believe that it's not a vulnerability. However, it's possible that it's a legitimate issue.
3. Determine the toxicity level and gauge the appropriateness of the responses. If the triager is too hostile or afraid to speak up, both scenarios have the potential to damage future interactions.
4. Provide commentary. Don't be afraid to give the triager more information to help them or to correct the course of action the triager is planning on taking. Perception is subjective. Therefore, program managers should be willing to express an opinion on the matter.
5. Intervene where necessary. If the situation appears to be negative to the point of no return, if it hasn't already occurred, inform the triager that it would probably be a good idea to remove the researcher from the program. Additionally, if misinformation about the state of the enterprise bug bounty program is being relayed from the triager, correct it. Starting with a private conversation is the best route to avoid any potential of accidentally embarrassing the triager. A simple, "I noticed that you said 'x' to the researcher and that's not exactly what we do" can be a saving grace for the communications between triage, the enterprise, and researchers.
6. It's possible that a triager can verify a vulnerability and then the interaction may turn sour with the program manager. In this instance, refer to: "Toxic Interaction #2" in Section 10.4 for guidance on resolution, keeping in mind that managed services should be brought into the loop before attempting to manage the disrespectful behavior with the researcher.

10.4   In-house Programs

Toxic interactions can intensify when enterprise bug bounty programs are operated without any form of managed service on a dedicated platform. It's no surprise that differences in opinion can occur between a program and a researcher, and program managers need to be aware of the various resolution options. With that being said, even though programs will ultimately have the final say, understanding where the researcher is coming from is part of the equation. However, a program should not allow themselves to be run over by a toxic security research who is displaying explicit or threatening behavior. As is the situation with false positives, dealing with a security researcher and addressing this situation can be difficult. In any case, two examples with explanations are provided to help spell out the importance of understanding and correctly addressing the situation.

Toxic Interaction #1

A researcher identifies what appears to be a remote code execution flaw against an enterprise. After careful consideration, the enterprise determines that the flaw is actually against the vendor's server and not their own. Additionally, the exploitation of this server does not expose the enterprise to risk, and there's no way of inadvertently affecting the enterprise in any way with this specific exploit. The program manager has verified that the case of exploitation is null, and responds to the researcher:

Note: The following situations are raw and have adult language to represent the true nature of toxic behavior that a program manager may experience.

PROGRAM MANAGER: After reviewing your report, we've determined that the remote code execution vulnerability is actually against one of our third-party vendor's assets, not ours. No data exposure or impact is occurring to our services. We know that some security researchers depend on money acquired from vulnerabilities. Therefore, we will let you coordinate with the vendor. The third-party vendor who manages the server that you had found is "x" and their website or contact is "x" – please contact them. We believe that they have a bug bounty program.

SECURITY RESEARCHER: No, this is absolute nonsense. I find remote code execution on your server and this is how you treat me? Look at the subdomain. It belongs to your company.

PROGRAM MANAGER: I completely understand your frustration, but that is simply not the case at all. If you use the commands "whois" and "nslookup" on the server that you found, you will see that the server does not belong to us at all. We don't own that server, and it does not interact with our services.

SECURITY RESEARCHER: Your company is full of bloody con artists. Do you think this is acceptable? I'm going to tell everyone on social media that you're bloody scammers. This is your server. I know it's your server. You just don't want to pay me. How many bloody researchers have you stolen research from? Do you think I wouldn't call you d*ckwads out for this? Goodluck surviving the blast.

PROGRAM MANAGER: I know you feel as if there is strong evidence in your favor. Unfortunately, the technical facts remain: we don't own this server. We don't have any sort of integration or interaction between the enterprise and this server. While we can confirm that *we do* work with this vendor, the asset does not pertain to our program and would be considered out of scope even if it did belong to us (it doesn't). We highly recommend that you reach out to the vendor to report your findings. Additionally, we don't appreciate the hostility, and would ask that you please work with us in a respectful way or we will have to remove you from further participation in our program. We know that security researchers such as yourself put in a lot of hard work, but going forward we hope to work through this issue appropriately, and with mutual respect.

SECURITY RESEARCHER: Damn you! I'm not doing anything for you, or any of you stupid fools! You stole my research! You're a bunch of bloody thieves and I'm going to show everyone this report and tell everyone about your server. You're bloody burnt now, and there's nothing you can do about it. If I were you, I would keep a close eye on your Twitter and other forms of social media!

Summary

At this point, it's quite obvious that the program manager does not have the capacity to break through and change the security researcher's toxic behavior. The maximum point of escalation begins to occur when the researcher begins to threaten the program manager by stating that they will tell everyone and informing the program manager to keep a close eye on social media. These threats should not be taken lightly, and preparations should be made in order to respond to the public if necessary. First and foremost, the program manager should have a quick call or chat with the enterprise's social media manager to warn them of possible toxic interactions. In most cases, social media managers are expert in the art of responding or not responding to social media threats and will know how to manage this. Inform the social media manager of the situation, and feel free to show the enterprise social media manager the report and the violator's toxic behavior.

The program manager should also ask the social media managers to notify them if the security researcher's complaints begin to escalate into a situation that needs a different level of response and management, but for the most part, it's probable that the threats can be ignored. Program managers should also perform due diligence and have a quick call with or notify the vendor of the situation as a courtesy. Informing the vendor will give them a chance to monitor the asset for any malicious or unusually nefarious activity.

Toxic Interaction #2

During the week, a bug bounty program receives a report for a legitimate vulnerability. The program manager has confirmed that the vulnerability is a directory traversal vulnerability, which is normally rated high. The security researcher believes that this is a critical vulnerability. However, no confirmation of any highly sensitive files was revealed. Therefore, the program manager has paid the researcher and resolved the report as a high priority. The researcher isn't happy, and begins to fight with the program manager:

SECURITY RESEARCHER: Did you have a chance to review my report?

PROGRAM MANAGER: Yes, we reviewed your report, triaged it, and paid you for your participation. We appreciate your continued vulnerability report and we encourage you to keep researching!

SECURITY RESEARCHER: I don't understand, why was this marked as a high vulnerability rating? I can literally access the server's files.

PROGRAM MANAGER: In your proof of concept, you demonstrated the ability to access the /etc/passwd file. While we don't want threat actors to have the ability to access any files that reside on the server, the account that is reading the files (www-data) has extremely limited permissions, and we were unable to use this vulnerability to access any sensitive files on the server. However, we agree that it's problematic to have an exposed /etc/passwd file and the general nature of the vulnerability could result in sensitive data exposure at a further time, but as of now, we are rating it as a high.

SECURITY RESEARCHER: Are you serious? Do you legitimately think this is OK? This should be a critical. Has your company lost its mind?

PROGRAM MANAGER: We understand your frustration, and we are keeping an open mind. If you can prove further exploitation, we would be happy to raise the severity of this vulnerability.

SECURITY RESEARCHER: Whatever. I don't care. Bye.

Summary

Obviously, this scenario is far less toxic than scenario #1. However, program managers need to be prepared for any circumstance. At this point, the scenario isn't necessarily toxic enough to warrant the removal of the researcher from the program. Nonetheless, the program manager's best bet will be to keep this event in mind and monitor the asset closely until the vulnerability is patched. The program manager can notify the infrastructure team responsible for the server and inform them of the interaction to encourage a faster resolution time.

Overall, the scenarios presented should provide an adequate example of what a severely toxic interaction and a more mild one look like. Toxicity is about perception. Therefore, a program manager should always prioritize the safety of the enterprise and put all feelings aside when dealing with program communication affairs. If a program manager reacts adversely because of a negative interaction, it can further escalate the problem. Emotional intelligence is a difficult subject to approach in program management. Security researchers may not understand why their tone sounds threatening and bug bounty program managers must be prepared to deal with the possibility of such occurrences. In addition, many security researchers don't operate in English as a native language and some translations may be perceived as more hostile than they actually are. Make an effort to understand the researcher's point of view.

10.5 Blackmail or Possible Threat Actor

Toxic interactions may be hard to decipher from actual threats and, in the instance of a threat actor trying to exploit the enterprise, may lead to a lot of confusion. As a general guideline, unsolicited emails that seem exceedingly threatening should be forwarded to the legal team immediately for the next course of action. Conversely, if the person is asking for money for a bug, cautiously respond and ask if they would like to be invited to the bug bounty program. If they respond with a lot of hostility in what seems like a possible exploitation attempt, forward to legal immediately for further review. All threats should be treated equally, just as all emails reporting vulnerabilities that seem legitimate should be reviewed.

10.6 Public Threats or Disclosure

The most sensitive situation is when someone threatens the organization publicly. There are multiple scenarios that could potentially take place, and program managers should be prepared to deal with each one of them – or understand program management well enough to adjust to dynamic situations. Here are some of the possible ways a program can be at risk:

1. *Security researcher discloses unpatched vulnerability*: it's possible that a researcher may get overzealous and post about a vulnerability immediately upon reporting it or before it's patched. While the act alone does not constitute toxicity, asking the researcher to remove the vulnerability may result in toxic backlash. Program managers may attempt to reach out to the researcher directly if they feel comfortable. Legal should not need to be involved. Step up as the program manager and tell the legal department that you will deal with it. Communicate with the researcher and ask them if they would be willing to take the writeup down until the vulnerability is patched. If they refuse, don't seek to punish them but, instead, escalate the criticality of patching that vulnerability internally. The most important part isn't that the hacker disclosed but that the vulnerability exists. Get it fixed.

2. *Threat actor blackmails or discloses vulnerability*: if the attention of a program manager is brought to a vulnerability that is released to the public without regard for the enterprise, inform social media managers not to respond, and consult with legal on the next move. Document any evidence of the exploitation and review logs of the affected asset(s). Validating the vulnerability is also a nonnegotiable portion of this exercise. However, if the enterprise has an incident response team, they should be notified first and foremost, before exploring the data. However, *before* engaging with legal, or even the incident response team, please ensure that it's a legitimate blackmail attempt and not just a researcher angry about a lack of contact. Nearly all situations in which a vulnerability is being disclosed can be worked out, and most threats are a result of a frustrated hacker who has gone unheard.

3. *Security researcher threatens to disclose on Open Bug Bounty*: program managers may find that a security researcher attempted to contact them multiple times and there may have been an oversight. They may report the vulnerability through a website such as Open Bug Bounty which forcibly discloses the vulnerability after 90 days (industry standard). Program managers should attempt to contact the researcher using any information on file under their Open Bug Bounty account. If a response isn't received, the program manager should investigate the asset and vulnerability type in question and set an alert for the disclosure date reveal to see the exploitation methodology and resolve as soon as possible if it's serious enough. If possible, getting the researcher into the bug bounty program and getting them paid is a priority. Encouraging research is the mission of bug bounty program managers. Typically, when an event such as a report through Open Bug Bounty occurs, it's the result of a bug bounty program that's too inaccessible to hackers. Program managers may observe this occurrence if they run private programs.

4. *Security researcher threatens to disclose on social media*: typically, the disclosure that is threatened by security researchers on social media is far more mild than one of a threat actor. A situation as described would usually start as the researcher asking if someone has a contract for the enterprise and tagging them on Twitter, Facebook, or LinkedIn. If they don't receive a response, the urgency increases, and depending on the tolerance of the researcher, they may threaten to drop it publicly or switch to a more threat-actor-like release mode. Program managers are usually free to respond with a little less caution, and

just as the email intake process is done, invite the researcher to the bug bounty program. If they don't want to disclose the vulnerability to the enterprise, realize that there's probably a good reason for it. Is the program paying researchers well? Does the program force a nondisclosure agreement upon a researcher after reporting? On average, researchers want money and public disclosure. Offer both and you'll typically note a better response. If the researcher refuses, do not pursue them with a legal team – rather, aim to fix the vulnerabilities that are revealed. Some researchers can't be reasoned with, but one must communicate with them appropriately and not in a threatening manner.

10.7   Program Warning Messages

Security researchers are hackers, and curiosity can be their saving grace and their downfall at the same time. Security researchers typically practice anonymity, and this may include using a virtual private network (VPN). For example, the enterprise program scope may say, "Don't use automated scans." A good enterprise security program will use a web application firewall or other rate limiting and blocking options, and a security researcher who decides to use their real IP can get blocked quickly during testing, especially if scanning. In a perfect program management world, a security researcher will respect the scope and not use automated solutions. In all reality, it's not usually an issue. However, circumstances may occur during heavy production times or development cycles and software engineers may report a lot of errors. Program managers will have to come up with creative ways to block the traffic if they are not utilizing tooling that can prevent this type of behavior automatically. Even if the enterprise does have tooling, messaging may be necessary to get the point across.

10.8   Threat Actor or Security Researcher?

To be frank, the "Is it a threat actor or security researcher?" game is awful to play and mentally exhausting for the program managers and any other involved teams. Over time, bug bounty programs have attempted to innovate unique ways to deal with this situation, such as requiring a specific VPN connection pack to begin research or instructing the researcher to use a specific user agent or header. Unfortunately, that may work in some instances, but the more that is required of a researcher to begin, the more friction it creates and participation may dwindle, or these requirements may be ignored altogether. Creating a playbook in these circumstances can help address the issues quickly, whether it's a mental note or physical documentation.

First, ask the following questions:

1. Where are the issues occurring and are they contained?
2. Is there production impact and, if yes, how severe is it?
3. Does incident response need to get involved?
4. Do the requests follow any basic pattern (IP addresses, headers, requests, URL paths, etc.)?

As a general basis, some of the above questions can be used to start sifting through data and analyzing the differences. Here are two different examples and their suggested resolutions.

Example 1: Determined Researcher

1. Where are the issues occurring and are they contained?
   Software engineers have noticed a heavy pattern of SQL (structured query language) injection attempts against one of the web application's login forms and they have notified application security. The attack isn't contained and it's still going on.
2. Is there production impact and, if yes, how severe is it?
   Production impact seems minimal at this point but the software engineers are concerned about the errors that have been observed.
3. Does incident response need to get involved?
   It doesn't appear that incident response needs to get involved. However the situation is being closely monitored.
4. Do the requests follow any basic pattern (IP addresses, headers, requests, URL paths, etc.)?
   Further observation of the pattern identified that all of the traffic was coming from the same IP address, which was mapped to the same country: Turkey. The requests appeared to be commonly used payloads from SQLMap, a command line tool for checking sites for SQL injection. Additionally, a security researcher from Turkey has been reporting vulnerabilities to us recently.

Resolution
In this instance, it appears that a security researcher was participating in the program, testing in-scope assets. After comparing previous requests made by the researcher, it became obvious. The IP address can now be comfortably blocked in the WAF. Automated testing is against program rules. Sending a message to all of the researchers in the program is a useful next step.

Example 2: Source isn't determined

1. Where are the issues occurring and are they contained?
   One of the infrastructure engineers noted abnormal traffic among some of the web application search queries. It's still occurring.
2. Is there production impact and, if yes, how severe is it?
   No production impact, but marketing is worried that search analytics will be skewed. They are extremely worried and …
3. Does incident response need to get involved?
   At the moment, it appears to be a form of scraping which is normal for ecommerce, however we've notified them to be on retainer.
4. Do the requests follow any basic pattern (IP addresses, headers, requests, URL paths, etc.)?
   The requests seem sporadic, user agents, IPs, and everything in between seem to vary significantly. The URL path seems to be the commonly used search path.

Resolution

Rate limiting rules seem to be blocking some of these IP addresses but others seem success-ful. Nearly every aspect of the request other than the URL path seems to vary. The URL path cannot be blocked, as it would affect real users. Based on the requests, this does not seem like security research. Bot detection solutions will help in this case. At this time, res-olution is limited to observing for repeating patterns, gathering IP addresses, and blocking IP addresses as they come in if deemed malicious. Messaging security researchers through the program seems fairly unnecessary in the current state.

Situation #1 seems like a security researcher. In this instance, patterns appear to match behavior observed in the past. Situation #2 is more of a nefarious situation in which reaching out to secu-rity researchers will be unnecessary. The questions above are not to be treated as an incident response plan but as a means of understanding some of the various information that program managers should attempt to acquire to assist in making the process easier.

10.9 Messaging Researchers

At this point, when there's a pattern of disruption, it doesn't hurt to send out a program message to remind participating researchers not to perform disruptive testing. The reason it's a good idea to send a message to all of the researchers is to avoid singling out the particular researcher. Program managers should avoid the possibility of causing further issues or demotivating the security researchers. In addition, there's always a chance that the analysis is incorrect and baseless or incorrect accusations could damage enterprise rep-utation. If using an in-house bug bounty program solution, you may have to send a mass email with BCC depending on the setup. Most managed bug bounty platform solutions have messaging functionality built in.

10.9.1 Security Researcher Interviews

Bug bounty programs benefit greatly from the expertise that security researchers bring to the table with the vulnerability research that they conduct.

Jackson Henry

Jackson Henry is a 15-year-old security researcher and member of the hacking group Sakura Samurai. Henry consistently operates as a team player, always honing his hacking skills and attempting to better himself every day. Jackson, while young, is known for various research including his participation in hacking the United Nations and his CVE (common vulnerabilities and exposures) discovery of a cross-site scripting (XSS) vulnerability on Apache, one of his many notable exploits.

How did you get into bug bounty hunting?
The first time I saw someone hack a website with ease was my inspiration. After that, I was hooked and wanted to learn more. I was determined to learn as much as I could and apply that knowledge to help secure businesses. There's nothing like the feeling of finding a critical vulnerability after days or weeks of hard work. Some people hunt bugs for money, and others hunt for swag – I find that the feeling of finding bugs is a reward in itself.

What are some of the things you look for when choosing a good program to hunt on?
I tend to choose programs with a large scope. A larger scope means that there will be a wider attack surface, and I will likely find exciting assets to hunt on!

In terms of hunting, what's the most serious bug that you've found?
The most serious bug that I have been a part of investigating would be an exposed PHP debug bar that led to account takeover and leaked SQL credentials. The database contained hundreds of thousands of email addresses, and millions of spam emails.

Have you ever been told a serious bug had no impact, or was rated low or disqualified? How did you handle the situation?
Quite regularly. In a lot of bug bounty programs, it seems as if managers will find any excuse not to reward security researchers who submit vulnerabilities to them. I generally lean toward moving on to the next program instead of seeking a reward.

If you had to give one piece of advice to another aspiring bug bounty hunter, what would you tell them?
Just get out there, and go for it! You can read all of the books and watch all the tutorials, but the real skill and progression comes from actually getting started by hunting on bug bounty programs.

What was one thing that you wish bug bounty program managers knew?
I wish all bug bounty program managers knew that hackers have a true passion for our craft. I also want program managers to know that looking for any reason to not reward a hacker for a legitimate vulnerability can be disheartening to new hunters, discouraging them from future participation

Ifrah Iman
Ifrah Iman is an independent security researcher and part-time bug bounty hunter based in Pakistan. She has over three years of experience in web application penetration testing and is active on multiple bug bounty platforms. She is skilled in testing client side and business logic vulnerabilities. She reported and secured the Department of Defence, Ministry of Justice UK, Singapore government, various other online businesses and companies. She is also the Founder of SheSecPakistan, an infosec community for Pakistani women.

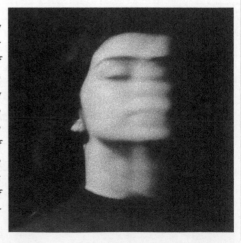

How did you get into bug bounty hunting?

I was fascinated by the concept of hacking after my high-school teacher taught us about viruses. I then started to experiment with tools like Cheat Engine to tweak PC games. Fast forward to 2017, I learned about the ethical side of hacking and reached out to other Pakistani people who were also interested in the bug bounty space. The bug bounty community has never denied me help when I've requested assistance, and I'm honestly grateful to the community for being so wholesome.

What are some of the things you look for when choosing a good program to hunt in?

I like to prioritize my time on programs with an interesting scope (wide or single site, I don't have a preference), suitable bounty range, and quicker response times.

In terms of hunting, what's the most serious bug that you've found?

Admin panel access leading to full takeover of the organization. I discovered a JavaScript (JS) file located in the source code of the login page for the admin panel which contained the editor's credentials. I was able to escalate the privilege of this bug because the admin panel was vulnerable to IDOR (indirect object reference). I was able to perform admin tasks from the editor's account.

Have you ever been told a serious bug had no impact, or was rated low or disqualified? How did you handle the situation?

Yes, on many occasions, serious bugs that I had reported were downgraded in criticality. If my vulnerability rating was downgraded, I commented on the report again, stating why the impact was far more severe than the assigned rating. Alternatively, I have reached out to the bug bounty platform provider directly in an attempt to resolve the problem. If my attempts don't get the severity upgraded, I move on and continue hacking, in an attempt to identify more vulnerabilities.

If you had to give one piece of advice to another aspiring bug bounty hunter, what would you tell them?

Invest time in learning and practicing, but also put your mental health first. If you're burnt out, take a break, reboot your mind, and then get back into the game.

What was one thing that you wish bug bounty program managers knew?

Bug bounties should be about allowing a hacker with an outside perspective to test their security. A program should actively work with hackers. Lack of communication between hackers and companies can lead to many critical findings being ignored. Additionally, program managers should attempt to reduce the amount of time it takes to triage, reward, and patch the vulnerability in order to reduce the number of duplicates.

Katie Paxton-Fear

Katie is a PhD student in cybersecurity and machine learning. In her free time, she's a bug bounty hunter and an educational YouTuber. She started out hacking in June 2019 during a HackerOne mentorship program and now hopes to be a mentor to others, creating YouTube videos. In her videos, she attempts to bridge the gap between "I know what bug bounties are" and "bug bounty hunter", giving advice specifically tailored to bug hunting. She's now produced over 40 videos on bug bounty hunting for an audience of over 20 000 subscribers. Aimed at a beginner audience, the videos vary from finding your first bug, the "how to" of utilizing specific tools, and the various ways security researchers can find specific bugs in the differing vulnerability classes. During her time bug hunting, she's been to 4 HackerOne live events and has found bugs in some of HackerOne's biggest clients, including the US Department of Defense.

How did you get into Bug Bounty Hunting?

I applied for a mentorship program run by one of the bug bounty platforms, HackerOne, even though I didn't have much experience at the time beyond being somewhat unfamiliar with the concept. I was accepted and during the event I found my first two bugs, despite never having been familiar with bug bounties prior. A month or so afterwards I was invited again, this time to Las Vegas, NV, during DEF CON, at that event I found another two bugs. I've been hunting for just over a year and I've found over 30 bugs in organizations ranging from the Department of Defense to Verizon and Uber. I also run a YouTube channel with 20 000 subscribers teaching others how to get started in bug bounty hunting.

What are some of the things you look for when choosing a good program to hunt on?

As a hacker, I want to work with organizations who want to work with me. I specifically look for organizations that have a good reputation with the hacker community or who have good communication statistics. I also like to work with targets I'm familiar with, or whose products I am already a user of. Sticking to targets or products I'm familiar with reduces the time taken to learn how an application works. I find that interesting targets such as a product with new features, a government organization, or technology I am interested in learning maintain a similar appeal. Additionally, I like to focus on one type of bug bounty hunting (such as API hacking), so a scope that includes APIs is also a draw. I read a lot of disclosed reports to better understand my target, so having a public program with disclosures on is something that I look for, specifically in looking at the communication between researcher and program.

In terms of hunting, what's the most serious bug that you've found?

Changing the runway length of an airport. On the face of it, a very simple bug, but the impact if it were not checked could have been huge. A longer runway is able to accommodate larger planes, which need the length to slow down on land. If the length of the runway is set to be too short, this may cause a "go around," which is where a plane attempts to land and must take off again, or at the worst could have caused a potential plane crash.

Have you ever been told a serious bug had no impact, or was rated low or disqualified? How did you handle the situation?

I'm inclined to believe that a program challenging the impact of a vulnerability happens less to those who are more familiar with the internal system. One of the challenges of bug bounty hunting is that we as hackers only see a small portion of an internal system. A hacker may misunderstand the impact because of the lack of internal visibility, especially if they are in a rush. In my experience, I've simply stated the impact that I believe exists, and if they disagree, the report will not be argued. However, the breakdown of impact agreement in this situation is often caused by a lack of communication. Program managers can manage the process by simply explaining to a bounty hunter, "This is why this isn't an issue from our side," which will lead to more friendly relationships if disagreements occur in the future.

If you had to give one piece of advice to another aspiring bug bounty hunter, what would you tell them?

Bug bounty hunting isn't a get-rich-quick scheme. When new bug bounty hunters first start out, they need to understand that they will not get rich or progress as quickly as they may hope to. The process of improving a hacking skillset takes time and patience. It takes practicing every day and hacking real targets. Participating in bug bounty programs definitely opens up the possibility to make money, of course, but at the start, bug bounty hunters will have to find their niche.

What was one thing that you wish bug bounty program managers knew?

Bug bounty hunters do actually care about internal processes, and want to know about the status of a bug, even if the update is as simple as, "This has been added to our internal tracking system." Most of the time, relationships between a bug bounty hunter and an enterprise bug bounty program break down as a result of a lack of communication between the parties. Being open about what's happening during the vulnerability remediation process will save a lot of unnecessary "any status update" comments from bug bounty hunters, and potentially help mitigate angry hackers, who often feel unappreciated due to lack of communication.

10.9.2 Bug Bounty Program Manager Interviews

Sajeeb Lohani

Sajeeb Lohani is a platform security engineer at Bugcrowd, who graduated with honors from Monash University with a bachelor's degree in software engineering (hons.) in 2017. Sajeeb also teaches web security for master's students at Melbourne University. Sajeeb holds OSCP and OSWE. Passionate about contributing to and improving cybersecurity research, Sajeeb currently holds more than 120 CVEs and is also a core contributor and co-developer of Interlace, a popular open-source project used for organizing and automating penetration testing workflows. As we go to press, Sajeeb is also ranked within the top 50 of BugCrowd

(#35) and within the top five of DVuln (#4). Sajeeb gives back regularly to the Melbourne cybersecurity community and is the founder of the Monash Cyber Security Club. Additionally, Sajeeb regularly presents at local meetups, and conferences. He mentors at the Australian Women in Security Network (AWSN) cadets workshops. Sajeeb also runs initiatives which attempt to responsibly disclose security issues within open-source software projects, with the vision of making the world of software "more secure." Sajeeb is also an active bug bounty participant and is proud to be listed in the hall of fame for Amazon, Yahoo, GitHub, Atlassian, Netgear, Okta, Spotify, AT&T, US Defense, and many more. Recently, Sajeeb was invited to an exclusive bug bash event for Okta, where he notably placed second among a field that included some of the most talented hackers in the world. Sajeeb has also presented in many renowned conferences, including DevSecCon Seattle, Bsides Perth, RuxCon, OWASP NewZealand, and many more.

How did you end up getting into application security?

I started off studying software engineering at Monash University. I was always fasci-nated by the vast world of information security and got my first chance to give it a shot during my second year working for Australia Post. After switching through many differ-ent companies (for around five years), and primarily working as a penetration tester, I am now the owner of the Bugcrowd bug bounty program and manage parts of our internal security.

In terms of triaging vulnerabilities, what does your workflow look like?

The program I run is a managed bug bounty program, implying that the Bugcrowd tri-age team helps with the triaging effort. I jump into the queue occasionally to help out. However, I usually wait for them to perform the "first touch" and tag me if they need extra help. After the bug is triaged, I'll perform a quick assessment to analyze the severity (basically checking if I need to wake people up and light a fire, or deal with the issue following standard service level agreements, or SLAs). After the vulnerability is triaged, I'll ping the required internal team and coordinate the effort required to patch the vulnerability.

Have you ever had an instance of a low- or no-impact bug in which a security researcher had argued with you? How did you resolve the miscommunication?

The situation of a vulnerability miscommunication is one in which every bounty program runs into eventually. Most of the time, providing proper justification of the decision is enough. If needed, I might end up providing transparency around the internal discussions. When the method of providing transparency doesn't work out, the Bugcrowd escalation team handles the situation. The escalation team will usually have a chat with us (the program) about our decision, to verify the extent of the situation. If our decision isn't incorrect, they advise us to overturn the decision made (no hard feelings there!). Otherwise, they reiterate our decision in a more consumable format.

If you had to give one piece of advice to other bug bounty program managers, what would it be?

Be transparent, show appreciation, help justify impact, and keep open communications! In the Bugcrowd program, we are quite transparent when dealing with issues. We are happy to dig into the fine details with researchers, attempting to uncover the under-lying issues and learn from the experience at the same time. We attempt to show our appreciation for good behavior, by providing perks such as great reporting bonuses, extremely creative attack bonuses, and privacy bonuses! We've seen a positive change in our program, after implementing unique rewards! Being a program owner allows for a far greater context of the internal workings of the applications. Attempting to help escalate the impact of a vulnerability or properly assess it is a great quality to have within a program. I believe that being on the lookout for potential points of escalation for a vulnerability attracts a lot more attention and makes the researchers want to come back for more! Finally, it really helps to keep simple and open communications with researchers. I personally achieve a far greater transparency by making myself known within multiple active Slack workspaces and Discord servers. I allow researchers to approach me about possible bugs to help them determine whether they should submit an issue, or if the issue is actually a regular occurrence. Allowing transparency and direct contact helps add to the credibility and accessibility of the bounty program.

What's one thing that you wish security researchers participating in your program knew?
Impact is everything. We try to identify the impact for you and escalate the bug, so that you can get the maximum payout. However, it's extremely necessary that researchers identify this themselves, as most programs won't bother doing that. I only know of a handful of programs that will. Finally, prompt and polite communications go a long way! I've personally provided bonuses to people purely because the experience dealing with them was easy and enjoyable. Please try to be patient and polite.

Geoff Galitz

Geoff Galitz has been in the technical infra-structure and security sectors for many, many moons. Really ... many. A great many. From small startups to enterprises and large academic environments he's happiest learning new technologies and topics ... which makes infosec and cybersecurity a natural fit.

He's contributed in various capacities to security-related projects over the years, including Snort (IDS), OpenVAS, Atomic Red Team, education programs, workshops, security awareness, and more.

You can reach Geoff via:
email: geoff@galitz.org
web: https://galitz.github.io

How did you end up getting into application security?
I consider myself more on the systems side, but I've certainly had my fingers in all sorts of fields and subfields over the years. I got into this security thing during my time at UC Berkeley. Being a high-profile research university, we were under constant siege from attackers. And being an open network, it was easy pickings. It was a matter of survival

that we had to take up cybersecurity or application security (or whatever you want to call it) just to get our work done. Since universities in those days had no real firewalls at their ingress points, systems would get hacked quickly. The fastest I saw was one box being hacked within 18 hours of it being installed and brought online. Just imagine that, some poor PhD student trying to get his or her computer jobs done by deadline in order to get that degree just to have their system compromised and yanked from the network by my team. Twenty years of school with the end just in sight just to be sunk by a hack from some kid hundreds or thousands of miles away. Ouch!

In terms of triaging vulnerabilities, what does your workflow look like?
I'd give the bug bounty report a good look over and then whip out curl or burpsuite or something similar to reproduce the issue. We'd typically loop in the developers no matter what the outcome of my test was. The devs could comment more authoritatively on the likelihood of a successful attack since they were closer to the subject matter. My job was mostly as a coordinator and negotiator.

Without compromising the integrity of your program or disclosure processes, what is the most serious bug that you've seen?
I have two of the same type that I'll talk about. The first was that an application that was public facing was decommissioned or moved elsewhere. However, the inbound NAT IP was never removed. Then another system came online and assumed the inbound target IP of that network address translation (NAT). So a critical infrastructure system ended up being publicly exposed. The second was essentially the same thing, but it was only for testing and, of course, the team forgot to remove that testing rule and a critical service was exposed publicly for several days before it was caught. That also goes to show that when designing bug bounty programs you should consider more than just XSS and SQLi and so on.

Have you ever had an instance of a low- or no-impact bug in which a security researcher had argued with you? How did you resolve the miscommunication?
We see some level of that constantly. Usually a simple reply along the lines of "That is mitigated by X" works. It has been pretty civil and polite for the most part. Consider that our bounty program was private when I was on it, so there was already some level of trust.

If you had to give one piece of advice to other bug bounty program managers, what would it be?
Remember that these researchers come from all sorts of different backgrounds with varying levels of language, cultural, and technological sophistication. Never assume any documentation, instructions, or expectations will be 100% clear all the time and try to be patient when things look like they are going sideways. Nobody gets into this to be difficult. Some of these folks are at a crossroads where this kind of work will set them on a positive path in life – try to be supportive of that. All the while they are helping you find the issues in your systems. You are doing each other a favor.

What's one thing that you wish security researchers participating in your program knew?

The researchers should know that the people they are dealing with at any organization are often caught in the middle. They have engineers and managers to deal with and not all of them are going to agree on prioritization or impact. I'd say the old axiom of don't shoot the manager goes both ways. We are all juggling the various things being asked of us.

Jesse Kinser

Jesse Kinser is the chief information security officer at LifeOmic, a precision healthcare company focused on improving patient care. She has written and presented her security research at leading security conferences around the world, such as DEF CON and RSA. Jesse's career has led her through a wide variety of security landscapes as she has worked for the US government, leading SaaS (software as a service) companies, and a few startups. Today Jesse wears multiple hats, leading LifeOmic's security program by day and hacking against other companies at night.

How did you end up getting into application security?

I studied information security during my undergrad life and then went on to work in the cybersecurity field after college. I really enjoyed the challenge of application security because it requires you to always be up on the latest technology and implementations. Developers are constantly changing how they build (or misconfigure) things and it keeps me engaged.

In terms of triaging vulnerabilities, what does your workflow look like?

We take a look at every report that comes in, sometimes even before our managed triage service reviews, which allows us to make sure the reports are prioritized internally and actioned quickly. If we notice a report looks like the hacker may be on to something but they are not quite there, we either give the hacker some guidance on where to keep digging or we dig deeper ourselves. If we uncover an issue internally based on the fact we only discovered it because a hacker report pointed us in the right direction, we still honor the bounty and award the hacker. Sometimes bugs just take teamwork.

Without compromising the integrity of your program or disclosure processes, what is the most serious bug that you've seen?

We have hackers primarily test against our dev instances of the products. This allows us to identify and catch bad bugs before they make it to production. In one instance, we invited hackers to test a new service before launch that was running on AWS Lambda. A hacker found multiple ways to exploit a serverless function that allowed them to obtain an AWS key. Luckily, we have many controls in place that rendered the key useless, but it was awesome to see the creativity the hacker came up with for serverless remote command execution.

Have you ever had an instance of a low- or no-impact bug in which a security researcher had argued with you? How did you resolve the miscommunication?
All the time. It's important to always explain the compensating controls your organization has in place that made you determine that it was low/no impact. Impact is a two-way street. If programs want impactful bugs, they must give hackers impactful information to help them along the way. If a hacker knows the controls in place that made you determine it didn't have any impact, they can then use that information to attempt to find a bypass, thus increasing the criticality of their efforts.

If you had to give one piece of advice to other bug bounty program managers, what would it be?
You can never communicate too much. Always engage and share as much information as you possibly can with hackers. Real-world attackers have endless time and resources and will find out the information regardless, so you might as well share that helpful knowledge with those hackers that are trying to help you be more secure.

What's one thing that you wish security researchers participating in your program knew?
We are open to feedback and always looking to make the program better. We view our bug bounty hackers as an extension of our security team, so if you are hacking on our program, you are one of us.

10.10 Summary

When it comes down to it, the bottom line is this: security researchers and program managers are similar. They all know that communication is an important aspect of program participation and management. Particularly, security researchers just want to be understood – they want their impact to be heard and assessed in a fair way. Program managers want the researchers to let them in and to let their guard down a bit more so that the situation can be assessed properly. In addition, they don't want to have to tell researchers to respect them: they just want to deal with patient researchers who are polite.

As both a security researcher and a bug bounty program manager, I have seen both sides of a wide array of issues. Ultimately, I know that I've been impatient as a researcher and that I've also been lax and not willing to hear a researcher out when operating as a program manager. When I catch myself doing these things, I readjust. There's no harm in admitting fault and adjusting stance – or even just realigning silently. Program managers and security researchers will appreciate adjustments, and that's what matters. Communication is a key component and driver.

Part 6

Assessments and Expansions

11

Internal Assessments

11.1 Introduction to Internal Assessments

Program managers, at a minimum, must understand why it's necessary to have a working understanding of penetration testing and the associated vulnerability assessment phases. Unfortunately, in some cases, enterprise leadership may not understand that program managers should have a background in application security with penetration testing, if not at least a working knowledge of application vulnerability types and mitigation processes. When an employee is hired with no knowledge of common vulnerability types, it may make managing the program exceedingly difficult. This chapter introduces some useful crash-course assessment concepts and tooling but the intention of this chapter isn't to replace formal penetration testing assessment resources. When reading through this chapter, please understand that penetration testing from both an application and network standpoint requires an extensive amount of training and practice. Some of the best penetration testers in the world still don't know every aspect of hacking. Aspiring hackers that want to up their game should seek other resources.

11.2 Proactive Vs Reactive Testing

The best bug bounty program managers don't begin testing after the vulnerability reports start rolling in. As can be said about a ship, one does not embark on a journey across the seven seas without checking the ship for holes and ensuring that it's sound and ready for smooth sailing. Program managers should perform full internal assessments before opening the program, even to a small group of security researchers. An amateur mistake would be assuming that one or even two security researchers would be an OK number of individuals to start with prior to testing. Enterprise assets need to be thoroughly hardened to prevent overpaying security researchers or forcing a pull-back of program launch. Regardless of all of the internal assessments performed, researchers will always find security issues, and program managers shouldn't be immediately alarmed when reports are received – even on assets that they have tested.

Corporate Cybersecurity: Identifying Risks and the Bug Bounty Program, First Edition. John Jackson.
© 2021 John Wiley & Sons, Ltd. Published 2021 by John Wiley & Sons, Ltd.

11.3 Passive Assessments

Arguably, one of the most important aspects of internal testing is to place oneself in the shoes of a threat actor. A malicious hacker does not automatically acquire a list of assets to attack. As does anyone else, a threat actor needs to perform reconnaissance to identify assets through various means. Program managers can benefit from understanding the different ways passive research is conducted, as it can open up a better understanding of security gaps, prior to performing any active testing at all.

Note: passive assessments require little/no interaction with the target. All IP address ranges and domains in this section are accessible to the public. Please acquire written permission to perform on any targets past the passive assessment stage. In fact, the intent of this book is to give program managers some tips and tricks to test on their own assets. It is not intended for use on nonprogram-related assets.

11.3.1 Shodan

The best way to describe Shodan is as a tool that turns active recon into passive recon. Shodan crawls the Internet continuously and attempts to identify open ports and services on those ports. It's a search engine that includes any Internet-connected device that it can make contact with. Program managers need to use Shodan as a resource because the enterprise may have exposed assets that they were not even aware of.

11.3.1.1 Using Shodan

1. First go to a browser and navigate to shodan.io (Figure 11.1).

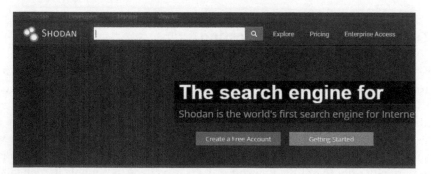

Figure 11.1 Shodan Browser Search.

Program managers will be greeted with a search bar and various functionality. Creating a free account is highly recommended, especially if this source will be used often.

2. In the search bar, type the IP address of the specific asset that needs to be looked up to see if Shodan has any data on it. In any case, a good course of action for a program manager

performing recon for the first time is to enter the name of a web application domain that is controlled by the enterprise, and click the magnifying glass to search (Figure 11.2):

Figure 11.2 Shodan Search Bar.

3. The search will then bring up a list of many different results (Figure 11.3). The domain may show up as linked to various assets, filtering by country, services, organizations, and products. At this point, any of this information is considered open and exposed to the Internet. Viewing the information isn't illegal in any sense. Program managers should be advised that it would be in their best interests to carefully check assets and ensure that they belong to the organization before proceeding with testing. Additionally, Shodan has a wide array of filters and logic that could be used. For example, a security researcher, threat actor, or program manager may want to obtain visibility on where a service is being used, or even a specific version of the service. In this scenario, we are using "vsftpd 2.3.4" as a means of searching and generating results.

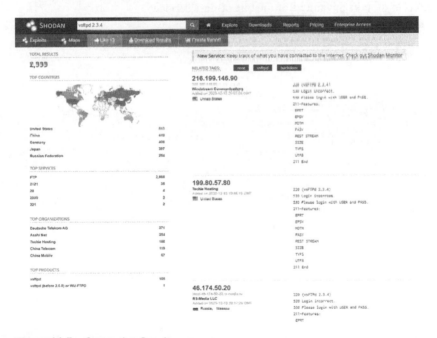

Figure 11.3 Generating Results.

4. Next, if an asset meets the criteria defined, a program manager can click on it to understand the impact and analyze enterprise exposure. Imagine that the asset labeled "216.199.146.90" appears to belong to the enterprise. When a program manager clicks on it, a new page loads that highlights many additional pieces of information including all open ports that Shodan has identified – as well as services, and the best attempt of identifying vulnerabilities against the asset based on versioning (Figure 11.4). It's important to note that some CVEs against services and versions may not be identified. Nonetheless, the level of insight that Shodan provides can prevent deadly situations.

Figure 11.4 Shodan Asset Analysis.

Taking a closer look at the vsFTPd 2.3.4 example (Figure 11.5), it can be seen that Shodan has appeared to confirm that this asset is running the service. If a program manager were to find out that one of their assets were running this version of FTP, it could mean that threat actors may be able to easily see this information too and, knowing that many exploits exist, take advantage of the out-of-date service.

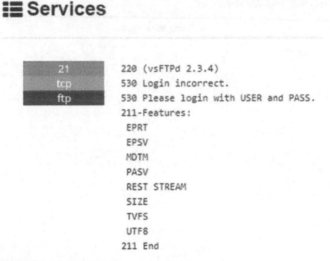

Figure 11.5 Shodan Services Analysis.

5. The risk identification process is essentially broken into several parts while using Shodan.

- Looking up assets by domain or IP address.
- Checking to see what information or additional mapping Shodan has on the assets.
- Identifying out-of-date versioning on services or infrastructure.
- Searching for exploitability.
- Confirming asset ownership.
- Attempting exploitation or relaying the vulnerability to the affected team.

For example, in this instance a program manager may not know what, if any, exploits exist against the various services or exposed ports. A quick Google search for "vsFTPd 2.3.4" brings up multiple well-known and developed exploits (Figure 11.6):

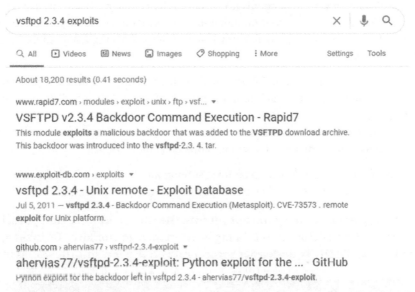

Figure 11.6   Google Search Results.

If the asset is indeed confirmed as belonging to the enterprise and it's verified to be running that service, a program manager now must contact the affected team immediately for resolution as the exploit could lead to a threat actor achieving remote code execution on the server. Shodan can help assist program managers in quickly identifying easily exploitable services and out-of-date components or assets that may have not been known about prior.

11.3.2   Amass/crt.sh

Common misconceptions presented by program managers are that "they know the extent of the subdomains controlled by the organization." Bug bounty program managers would be surprised to find that infrastructure teams have abandoned subdomains that are actively hosting applications and exposing them to the Internet or creating unnecessary risk. Amass provides far more functionality than just subdomain enumeration. However, a quick technique exists to help program managers quickly identify subdomains passively in order to look for additional attack surfaces.

Additionally, crt.sh is a tool that can be used to gather more subdomains and to possibly enumerate technology that the organization is using. crt.sh looks for all certificates containing variations of the root domain provided, which can be helpful (and even surprise a program manager). Domains not found before enumeration can be dumped into Amass (although it's important to note that Amass also performs queries from crt.sh) or a preferred subdomain enumeration tool to discover even more assets to test on.

Special thanks to Donk for showing me crt.sh (Twitter: @donk_enby).

11.3.2.1 Amass

As a standard, Amass comes standard with Kali Linux or most other penetration testing distributions. First and foremost, gather a list of domains that need to be tested. As a program manager, maintaining a list of all of the subdomains is a necessary evil, or in other words, no subdomain oversight equals no vulnerability oversight. If the enterprise is large enough, acquiring a list of all root domains may be difficult. If the organization is using Amazon Web Services (AWS), talk to infrastructure or networking teams to make a determination of all assets.

1. First, put all of the root domains in a file, such as example.com, example2.com, etc. Once this is done, dumping subdomains into the file can be an additional method of testing as results may prove to be promising.
2. After the domains/subdomains are in a file, run the subdomain enumeration with Amass: amass enum -df test.txt > subdomains.txt (Figure 11.7)

The above command tells Amass to perform subdomain enumeration on the domain/subdomain file with the -df switch; it then writes the output into the subdomain file (Figure 11.8).

Note: if having issues writing the output into the file, make sure that permissions are correct on the directory that is being written to. Additionally, if Amass appears to stall at a specific DNS queries per second rate after a few minutes, stop the tool.

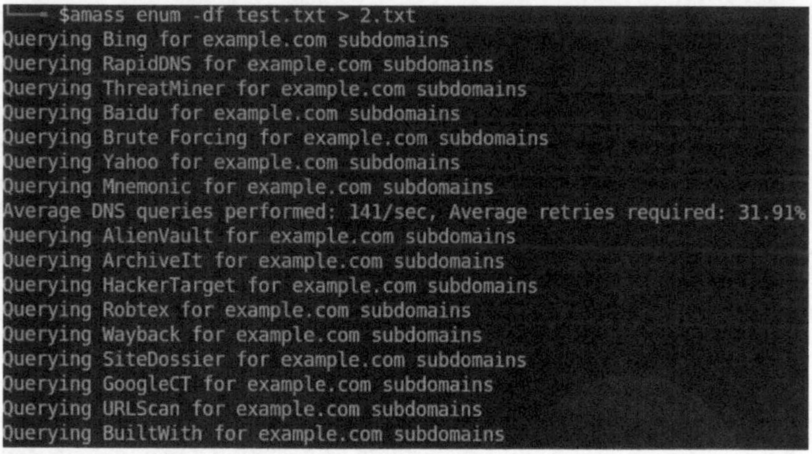

Figure 11.7 Amass Scanning for Subdomains.

Once the tool is finished, subdomains will be output into the file specified.

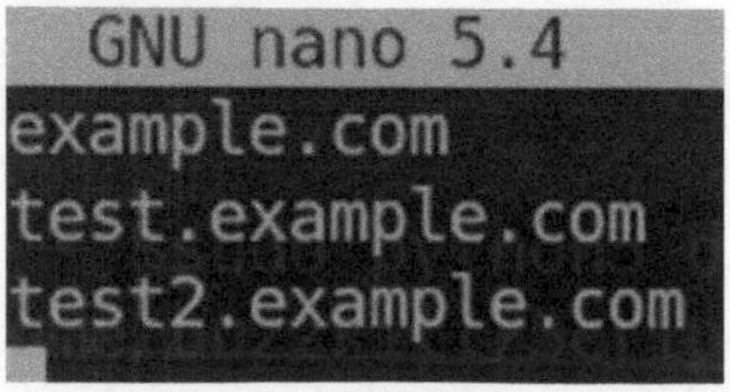

Figure 11.8 Subdomains in Nano.

11.3.2.2 crt.sh

Subdomain enumeration is an essential portion of testing. Even though Amass queries crt.sh, program managers may want to see a more comprehensive overview on the certificates and software utilized. Utilizing crt.sh is a fast alternative to using scans to discover domains that may have been overlooked (Figure 11.9).

Figure 11.9 Subdomain Enumeration with crt.sh.

11.4 Active Assessments

An active assessment is one in which a hacker tests for vulnerabilities. The active stage can be considered disruptive to the enterprise if a program manager is not careful. Extreme caution should be exercised and no exploitation attempts should be made in the instance that a program manager is inexperienced. It is highly recommended to be comfortable with exploitation before moving into this phase as it can be detrimental to the production environment. Even when comfortable with exploits, a good practice is to inform the organization via a "Pentest" active board or post somewhere to let everyone know to contact you if any weird traffic comes their way. Doing so can prevent an "all hands on deck" emergency-type situation. Plenty of tooling exists for active testing. However, only several small aspects will be covered (more automated tooling for the busy professional).

11.4.1 nmapAutomator.sh

Nearly any beginner hacker understands nmap, but how about nmapAutomator? The tool was designed by 21y4d and can be found on GitHub. It was created as an easier means of combining multiple toolsets for network and web application hacking, including full nmap port and service scans on tcp/udp, CVE scans, and following that, various suggested recon commands depending on the ports/services found. Additionally, nmapAutomator will utilize nikto, gobuster, sslscan, joomscan, wpscan, droopescan, smbmap, smbclient, enum-4linux, snmp-check, snmpwalk, dnsrecon, ldapsearch, odat, etc. The tool can be used for a wide variety of scenarios, but is best used on backend servers.

Figure 11.10   nmapAutomator Scanning Information.

As can be seen in Figure 11.10, there are many options to use in conjunction with nmapAutomator. Program managers can utilize the command **./nmapAutomator.sh 10.0.0.212 All** to perform a full scan on the asset. Once the command is executed, the tool will go through various stages including a quick scan, basic scan, and full scan (Figure 11.11), and then evaluate the given services to perform more refined tool usage and vulnerability scans thereafter. All of the results will be output into a folder to enable a neat and organized way to maintain findings (Figure 11.12).

Figure 11.11   nmapAutomator Performing Full Scan of Asset.

Figure 11.12   nmapAutomator Results.

11.4.2 Sn1per

Created by 1N3, Sn1per is yet another automated vulnerability scanning tool. A free version of Sn1per can be downloaded from GitHub. However, a professional version that allows a graphical user interface (GUI) view and workspace management is available. The free version can be utilized efficiently. Once the tool is downloaded and configured per the instructions, a program manager can take a URL for a domain and begin testing against it. Sn1per has a lot of modes. However, a good start would be the utilization of the "normal" mode.

Once downloaded, it's as easy as utilizing the command: **sniper -t https://example.com**.

The tool will then attempt to utilize a wide variety of enumeration tools on the domain for both web application and network penetration testing. Be warned: if not specified, the tool may attempt various exploits which could be detrimental to the production environment; it's essential to be prepared for this instance. (See ures 11.13 and 11.14.)

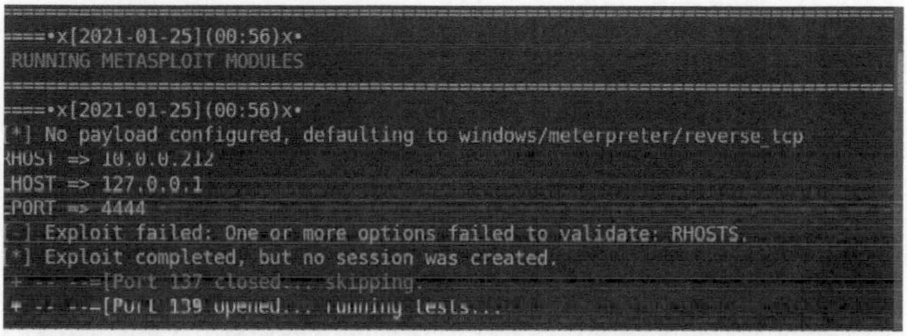

Figure 11.13   Sn1per Running Metasploit Modules.

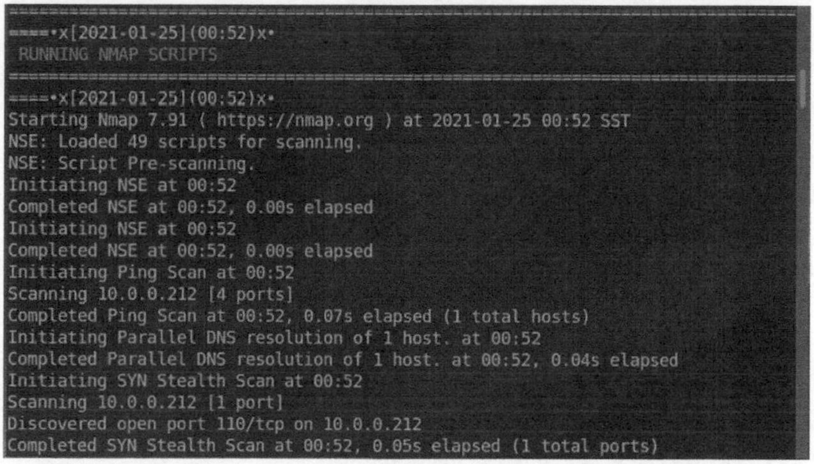

Figure 11.14   Sn1per Running Nmap Scripts.

11.4.3 Owasp Zap

In the suite of free DAST (dynamic application security tools) is OWASP ZAP. This tool focuses on the aspects of web application testing, and will evaluate URLs or parameters for a wide range of vulnerabilities. ZAP comes with most penetration testing toolkits, including Kali Linux and Parrot. Alternatively, the professional version of Burp Suite has a decent DAST scanner. However, not every program manager will have access to the funds to purchase a license.

Scanning is fairly easy: once the tool is loaded a program manager can input a URL in the "URL to Attack" field. At this point, it's as easy as pressing "Attack." However, in more realistic scenarios or depending on an enterprise's needs, the configurations may need to be modified. There are plenty of open-source guides that explain the many things that ZAP can perform when configured for advanced usage.

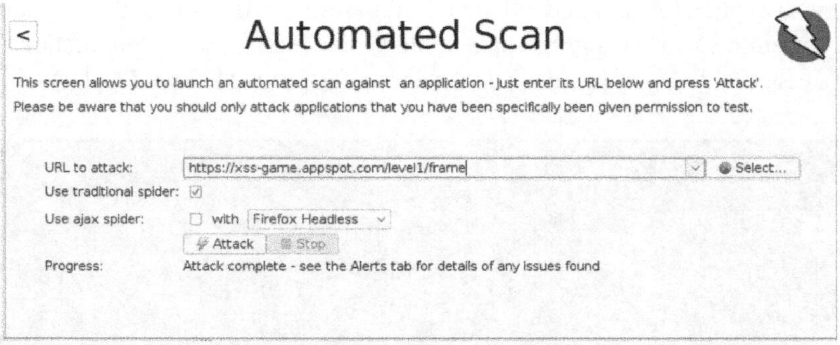

Figure 11.15 Setting up an Automated Scan in OWASP ZAP.

For the example shown in Figure 11.15, we are using a purposely vulnerable domain for testing purposes.

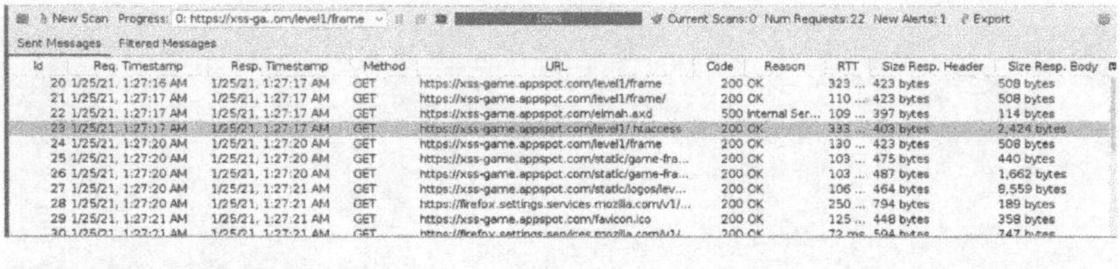

Figure 11.16 OWASP ZAP Scan Results.

When the "attack" button is clicked, it will begin to crawl and test a wide variety of payloads to look for vulnerabilities (Figure 11.16).

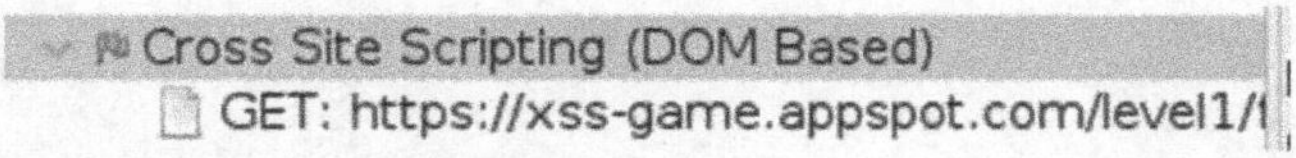

Figure 11.17 OWASP ZAP Potential Vulnerability Result.

The alerts fields shows all of the possible vectors of attack, and in this case the crawl and payload testing discovered a DOM Based XSS vulnerability (Figure 11.17). To the right of the vulnerability identified, a payload and description of the attack is typically available. If we copy the payload, it looks like this:

https://xss-game.appspot.com/level1/frame#jaVasCript:/*-/*`/*\`/*'/*"/**/(/* */oN cliCk = alert())//%0D%0A%0d%0a// </stYle/ </titLe/ </teXtarEa/ </scRipt/-! >\ x3csVg/ < sVg/oNloAd = alert()// >\x3e

When the payload is entered into the browser, a successful XSS attack is executed (Figure 11.18):

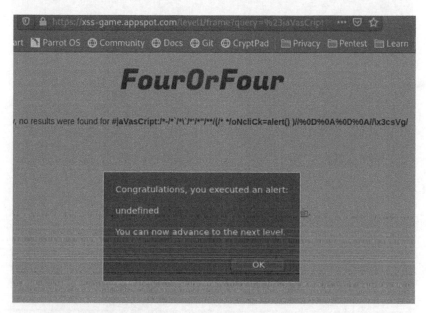

Figure 11.18 XSS Attack Performed.

Don't be fooled: OWASP ZAP isn't a dedicated XSS tool. It maintains the capacity to fuzz, edit and resend requests, and search for an entire slew of vulnerabilities. A program manager can spend hours customizing ZAP and can even export vulnerability reports.

11.4.4 Dalfox

One of the best tools in a program manager's arsenal for testing URL parameters and finding hidden parameters is DalFox. Maintained by hahwul, DalFox can be downloaded from GitHub. By gathering a list of URLs, or even having a list of root domains, DalFox has proven to be a worthy tool. The file option allows for testing multiple parameters, whereas a single URL can also be provided for testing (Figure 11.19). There are plenty of options to utilize, so please read the manual prior to usage.

For this specific example, a known vulnerable URL will be utilized from our previous testing with ZAP.

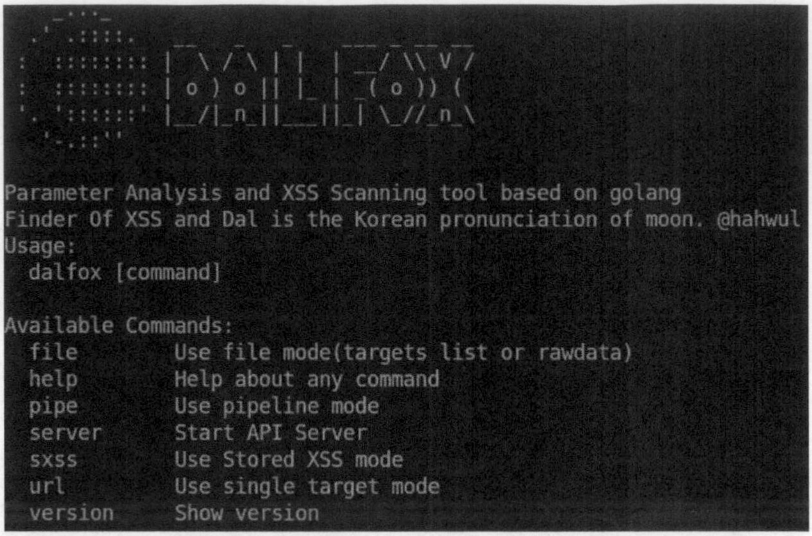

Figure 11.19 Dalfox Available Command.

/dalfox url https://xss-game.appspot.com/level1/frame

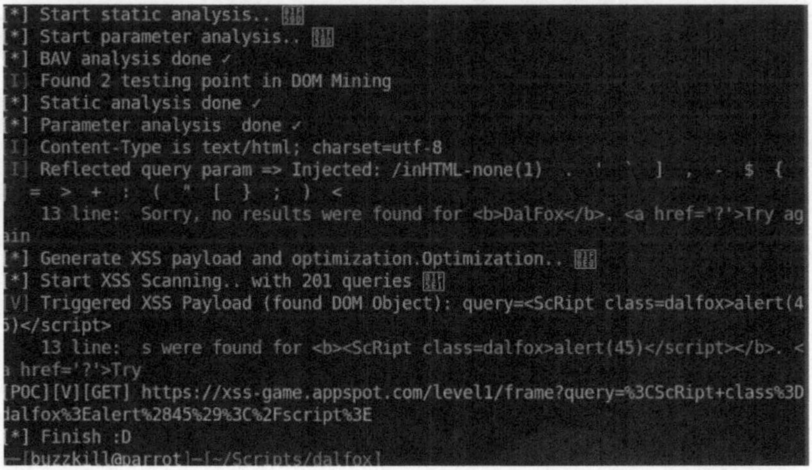

Figure 11.20 Dalfox Identifying an XSS Instance.

Quickly after running the script, an XSS instance is identified via the query = parameter (Figure 11.20). A final payload is output with a [POC][V] meaning that the exploit was verified as working – or at least detected as such (Figure 11.21).

Payload: https://xss-game.appspot.com/level1/frame?query=%3CScRipt+class%3Ddalf
ox%3Ealert%2845%29%3C%2Fscript%3E

Figure 11.21   XSS Attack.

11.4.5   Dirsearch

Fuzzing is an important aspect of internal assessments as well. Hackers love to jump to the
meat and potatoes of exploitation, which leaves many to forget that, sometimes, more is
less. The best attack is one in which the hacker knows everything there is to know about
the target. Therefore, program managers should strive to know twice as much as the participating security researchers. The idea of fuzzing is to search for secret files or directories
on a web application. Dirsearch simplifies the process. As most of the tools, starting
requires downloading it from GitHub, unless it's prepackaged with the penetration testing
operating system of choice. Dirsearch was created by maurosoria. Once again, reading the
manual is important as there are plenty of different switches to create and fine tune the
involved processes.

Several combined switches seem to be effective for quick testing: -x to include status
codes to ignore false positives (or an overload of irrelevant true positives), -e to annotate
which extensions need to be tested, and -f to force append extensions onto each word tested
from the default wordlist. For example, if a URL were tested and the tool was looking for
an admin directory, admin.php would also be tested if utilizing "-e php –f" as a switch
option. If a more hasty test is utilized, removing the -e and -f switches will test directories
and include file paths only.

As an example, imagine the following command: python3 dirsearch.py
-u http://127.0.0.1:8000 -e php,txt,bak,conf -f -x 300,301,302,303,304,400,401,402,403,404,5
00,501,502,503,504

Given that 127.0.0.1 is the domain, such as https://example.com – and the semicolon is
either the preferred port or service (unnecessary to append the port for ports 443 and 80) –
the command will look for files and directories and output them along with the status
response code when finished (Figure 11.22).

```
Target: http://127.0.0.1:8000/

Output File: /home/buzzkill/Scripts/dirsearch/reports/127.0.0.1/_21-01-25_16-43-
02.txt

[16:43:02] Starting:
[16:43:03] 200 -    318B  - /.ICEauthority
[16:43:03] 200 -     51B  - /.Xauthority
[16:43:03] 200 -     7KB  - /.bash_history
[16:43:03] 200 -     5KB  - /.bashrc
[16:43:03] 200 -    776B  - /.cache/
[16:43:04] 200 -     2KB  - /.config/
[16:43:04] 200 -    234B  - /.dbus/
[16:43:05] 200 -    482B  - /.emacs
[16:43:06] 200 -    290B  - /.gnupg/
```

Figure 11.22   Dirsearch Finding Folders.

11.5   Passive/Active Summary

There's a wide range of tools available to program managers, and this portion of the book doesn't even scratch the service of the amount of free tooling and resources available, including the manual reviews that can be done to support the health of the bug bounty program. Program managers don't need to be expert hackers with impeccable wit and skill, but they do need to know how to identify low-hanging fruit, and a lot of the tooling discussed is good when utilized for the purposes of surface level penetration testing. Nonetheless, program managers should aspire to learn as much as possible to identify a wider range of bugs.

11.6   Additional Considerations: Professional Testing and Third-Party Risk

For program managers that don't have the experience to perform internal assessments themselves, they should outsource to a trusted penetration testing firm and ask for a black-box test (meaning no information is given). Even enterprises that have the expertise to carry out full penetration tests could benefit from further testing, especially if the engineers do not perform penetration testing as a full-time job. Third-party risk is yet another factor that needs to be considered throughout the assessment period. It's easy to think about the impact of testing company-owned assets, but how about assets not owned by the enterprise running the bug bounty program?

It would be unwise to open up a program to security researchers if the enterprise isn't prepared to deal with remediating a lot of vulnerabilities. Third-party risk can be yet another factor, opening up the opportunity of exploitation or more bugs that a program will have to pay if not recognized in the first stage of partnership from company to company. Program managers should work with governance, risk, and compliance to evaluate acquisitions or partners consistently. Failure to do so can result in the exploitation of the organization.

12

Expanding Scope

Earlier in the book, the scope of a bug bounty program was discussed and a key principle was to ensure that the scope that is defined was not too wide to prevent overburdening of the program managers who are attempting to triage and remediate vulnerabilities. The idea behind scope expansions is to give researchers more surface to test on. After all, a threat actor may want something that the enterprise has: scope does not exist in the world of crime and illegal personal gain.

Opening up additional assets for testing can prove painful if too many assets are added or if an enterprise decides to offer rewards on an untested asset. While there's not necessarily a right or wrong time to expand scope, several steps can be taken to mitigate the potential of failure, nearly all within the realm of prior testing and level of effort.

12.1   Communicating with the Team

The nonnegotiable aspect of scope expansion is adequately portraying intentions to the team. Standalone program managers should communicate with leadership to ensure that everyone is on the same page with the expansion. A program manager should never add an asset without talking to other engineers on the team. Bridging any gaps in communication is a fairly easy process, and with an adequate plan resistance won't necessarily be met unless the budget isn't flexible for the needs of the bug bounty program.

Program managers should focus on a few aspects to enable a thorough conversation:

- Intention: during the process, the reason for scope expansion should be discussed with the program team or with leadership. The idea of the expansion is to allow more attack surface. Therefore, the reasoning should be communicated to the appropriate party.
- Testing: let the team know what the vulnerability analysis plan is prior to the expansion. An in-house penetration test may suffice, but weighing the pros and cons of an out-sourced penetration test may be necessary depending on the attack surface. For example, expanding to one single subdomain may be a small project, whereas adding an additional root domain for a subsidiary company could prove to open up quite a large attack surface.

Corporate Cybersecurity: Identifying Risks and the Bug Bounty Program, First Edition. John Jackson.
© 2021 John Wiley & Sons, Ltd. Published 2021 by John Wiley & Sons, Ltd.

- Value: highlight the value of an expansion. At the point of considering such expansions, leadership should already have seen an adequate vulnerability finding and resolution workflow. Therefore, value should speak for itself. If the workflow has been less than ideal, considering an interim solution, such as adding more hackers to the program or achieving a better security posture, may be a better option.
- Target launch: talk about ideal scope expansion data. Notification is essential: there's nothing worse than surprised engineering teams. In addition, proper notification can assist in preparing the teams for the expansion, and in some cases development teams may be dedicated to monitoring and ensuring a smooth launch.
- Follow through: explain what the intention looks like for rolling back or putting a hard stop on the expansion if any issues occur.

12.2 Costs of Expansion

Program managers should never expect that an expansion, even to a single asset, will yield minimal results or payouts. Before expanding, it's absolutely essential to evaluate the current bounty pool and analyze the trends of payouts over the course of the period to attempt to get a rough estimate of what the expansion may do to the budget. Additionally, no expansions should occur if the budget is severely limited or if a program is close to hitting the maximum allotment for the fiscal year. If the enterprise is running a program that offers points instead of bounties, it's still essential to ensure that a thorough analysis of vulnerability reports submitted occurs to prevent burdening teams.

12.3 When to Expand Scope

Unfortunately, there's never a correct way to actually define this. There are most certainly best practices, but an actual enterprise program may have a wide array of considerations to take into account before being able to make a decision on an expansion. Ideally, scope expansions are best approached when there is adequate reason to believe that the current scope is either too limited or exhausted in one way or another. Take, for instance, an enterprise program that is receiving an average of five or more reports a month. Depending on the payout table for the program, over five reports may end up being a little more than the enterprise had bargained for and an expansion of additional assets may not be appropriate.

Expanding scope is about comparing the current reports received within a given period, and analyzing the enterprise's ability to prepare and safely increase the effectiveness of the program without inadvertently damaging the program. Program managers can find great solace in expanding when ready and not rushing into it.

12.4   Alternatives to Scope Expansion

Scope expansions aren't the only way to encourage more program participation. Program managers can alternatively invite more security researchers, with automated approaches and by hand. For example, most bug bounty management platforms have an option to send automated invites out to researchers until a certain threshold of reports is met on a monthly basis. Automated invites may increase the amount of reports that a program receives. If the amount of hackers being invited is abnormally high, it's best to remove the option and consider a scope expansion.

To elaborate, imagine that the enterprise has 120 security researchers. If after a few weeks, it's getting close to 200 and no reports have come in, it may be time to expand scope. Exhausted scopes can discourage security researchers. Overly restrictive scopes tend to have the same effect. Therefore, dynamic adaptations within program management need to be used when the program becomes stagnant.

12.5   Managing Expansion

The same processes that have been applied to the pre-considerations of setting up a program should be applied to scope expansions. Testing, communicating with teams and developing expectations with leadership are essential parts of this process. A program manager should not attempt to form any expansion processes until a baseline level of security is considered.

13

Public Release

13.1 Understanding the Public Program

Ultimately, the public program is the end state. Most legitimate bug bounty programs aspire to finally opening up their doors to everyone. As is any other expansion incentive, the biggest consideration is a matter of being prepared for this undertaking. A lack of preparedness or a premature launch can result in the complete obliteration of enterprise reputation. The public program is meant to be a way of giving anyone and everyone a chance to research. Many enterprises may never reach this state depending on the size of their program, but it's undoubtedly the final incentive that most will want to reach.

13.2 The "Right" Time

Regardless of the desired launch, there isn't exactly a right time to launch. The key principle is to not launch too early, to avoid issues with the team being overwhelmed. Thinking about whether an enterprise should open a program is more than just a standard yes or no. A public program means full transparency at all times, and even with a limited scope researchers typically manage to find a ton of vulnerabilities. Considering the various aspects of a public program launch is an absolute necessity:

1. Employees: does the enterprise have enough employees to manage the incentives if it gets busy? For example, if an application security team has three employees overseeing dozens of high-priority projects, it may become necessary to set up a separate dedicated bug bounty program team alongside them.
2. Analysis: has the entire program been through rigorous testing? In a scope expansion, only the added assets have to be tested, but prior to public launch, testing is needed to prevent paying out for a lot of easily identifiable vulnerabilities.
3. Team: is the entire team on board for the expansion? Does everyone realize their roles in their process and the level of effort and coordination needed?

Corporate Cybersecurity: Identifying Risks and the Bug Bounty Program, First Edition. John Jackson.
© 2021 John Wiley & Sons, Ltd. Published 2021 by John Wiley & Sons, Ltd.

4. Finances: does the enterprise have a flexible enough bounty pool in the event that a lot of high-impact vulnerabilities are reported quickly?
5. Statistics: how many hackers are currently within the program and how often are vulnerability reports received? Has scope been expanded multiple times prior to the public program being initiated?

While there are many more aspects that can be evaluated, the above highlights some pertinent questions that should be asked prior to such a big expansion. Program managers should take the time to be honest about their assessment to ensure that they do not sink the program by launching before the enterprise and the employees are ready to deal with the work.

13.3 Recommended Release

Managed services and account managers exist for a reason – utilize them. One thing is known for certain: an enterprise should not take a bug bounty program public until it can handle managing over 100 hackers and is prepared for a giant spike in reports. Managing the public release of a program requires diligent planning and careful execution, especially if the program belongs to a big-name company. The official recommendation is to release **when ready** and not based on a specific guideline. While having over 100 hackers seems to be a decent milestone, it may not equate to a prepared enterprise bug bounty program.

13.3.1 Requirements

To play it safe, program managers should aspire to check off all of these tasks:

- Have 100 active hackers participating in the bug bounty program.
- Receive multiple vulnerability reports weekly.
- Analyze the budget to ensure that the enterprise can ingest new costs and associated risks.
- Present an adequate plan of expansion to management.
- Explain any new workflow predictions to fellow colleagues or managed employees.
- Prep the software engineers for the release and inform the organization with a mass notice.

Ensure that, as a baseline, all of the above bullet points are met. In actuality, a program manager may have to adapt and should analyze **each and every** possibility.

13.4 Rolling Backwards

The reason it's important to express all of the necessary precautions is because a rollback of the launch of a public program isn't a great start. It can be detrimental to the security team because it's embarrassing, as well as the software engineers (depending on the issues that occur). For example, if a public program is launched and the reports are overwhelming, a program manager may end up rolling back the program as it may be the only way to catch up with all the reports, especially if underprepared or understaffed. Doing so can hurt security researchers and cause a lot of mistrust and paranoia about the status of their report. It's best to gather in all of the reports that were submitted prior to the closure of the public program to prevent unnecessary refute. Still, rolling a program back into private mode may be the only way to handle a situation in which a program manager wasn't prepared. Always have a backup plan.

13.5 Summary

To be frank, not every program manager will receive the opportunity to take their program public – especially if consistently underfunded and overworked. While the goal should always be to launch a public program, it may simply not be on the cards for a smaller asset with no capacity to manage such incentives. It's not necessarily a cut-and-dry requirement to have to push a program into a public state. Feel out the idea of taking the program public and maintain an effective private program for a while before deciding to do so.

Index